Ten Things I Wish I'd Known When I Was Younger

A Christian Life Perspective

Robert D. Smith, Jr.

ISBN 978-1-64114-011-9 (paperback)
ISBN 978-1-64114-012-6 (digital)

Christian Faith Publishing, Inc.
832 Park Avenue
Meadville, PA 16335
www.christianfaithpublishing.com

Printed in the United States of America

CONTENTS

AUTHOR'S NOTES

Unless otherwise noted, all scripture references in this book are taken from the New International Version (NIV) of the Bible.

Throughout the book's narrative and lyrics, I have chosen to adopt the convention of several Bible translations (among them KJV, NIV, and ESV) with respect to capitalization of pronouns referring to members of the Holy Trinity. Specific name references (for example, *God, Jesus, Holy Spirit, Father, Son, Savior*, and *Lord),* of course, begin with a capital letter while personal pronouns (for example, *he, him, his*, and *himself)* begin with a lower-case letter. I realize that this differs from some Bible versions and writing conventions and is by no means a sign of disrespect. My sole intent is to provide the reader a consistent and easy-to-read style of writing that conforms to common Bible versions.

Life's lessons often include stories, which invariably involve the participation of human beings. To respect the privacy of the living and the memory of those who have passed on to their eternal destination, I have avoided using people's names and refer to story characters with generic references such as friend, acquaintance, co-worker, col-

league, pastor, and other words describing my relationship with those people.

All song lyrics in this book are © 2000–2016 Bob
Smith. If you would like to experience the musical portion
of the songs, please search the web for any of the below
albums or visit one of my music websites:

www.message-songs.com
https://bobsmith.hearnow.com
www.cdbaby.com/Artist/BobSmith1
www.jango.com/stations/270602471/tunein

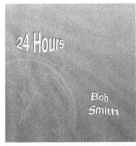

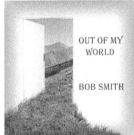

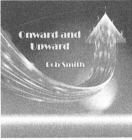

PREFACE

Let's face facts: we're all getting older. We're not old, mind you—just getting older. I am in my mid-sixties. To me, old is mid-seventies and beyond. Of course, when I have reached that milestone, Lord willing, old age will probably seem to me to be my eighties and nineties. One thing is for certain: I'm not as young as I used to be, and my body now and again reminds me of my advancing years. And so if we are never old and only perpetually getting older, there is always time left to learn and grow while we are on this side of the grass or flame.

It has been said that the benefits of aging are experience and, if we learn from our experience, wisdom. I agree wholeheartedly. Even as my body protests the aging process, my inner being is benefiting from decades of life experiences. My values, perspective on life, level of contentment, and assessment of what is important are much more mature than they were when, as songwriter Billy Joel sang, "I wore a younger man's clothes." You might say I am pretty comfortable in my own (albeit wrinkled) skin.

This book is not about what I've done in my life as most memoirs are. I've never been famous or notorious, so most people really don't care about my life story. This book is about what God has done in me and through me over the years and about the spiritual revelations I've had during the amazing experience we call life.

Over the last several decades, I have learned important lessons about the Christian life that I wish I would have learned earlier in life, hence the book's title. Sharing some of these lessons while I am still lucid enough to articulate them is my goal. It is my hope that nonbelievers believe and that believers move toward a deeper relationship with their Creator.

I mentioned Mr. Joel because, like him, I am a songwriter. I taught myself guitar and piano, at which point I taught myself the art of songwriting—both music and lyrics. In the mid-1980s, I wrote my last secular song and gave my musical endeavors to God. Since that time, I have written over one hundred fifty contemporary Christian songs, released ten albums, performed many concerts, and gained a fan following locally and around the world via Internet radio airplay. I've been quite successful at every aspect of music except becoming famous and making money. But those have never been my goals because for me, music is a ministry—a way of serving the Lord. And he has certainly blessed this ministry.

This book gives me the opportunity to share some of the lyrics that have been particularly meaningful to me and to others over the years. As my music website (message-songs.com) states, a song has the unique ability to convey a message—good or bad—to the listener in a very short period of time. The musical part of a song is not at all important to a person who is hearing impaired, yet the message carried in the lyrics can be.

When my music pastor at church introduces a hymn or song, he often talks about the writer, sharing inspirational stories of people like Fanny Crosby, Isaac Watts, and Horatio Spafford. When he does, he is always referring to the lyricist, not the composer of the music, though the two go seamlessly together. If one or the other were to stand alone in influencing lives, it would have to be the lyrics, which carry the all-important faith message. Therefore, you will find some lyrics relevant to the adjacent text scattered throughout the book.

Bette Davis said, "Old age ain't no place for sissies," and in terms of the body's inevitable decline, that's true. But I believe the aging process is a matter of attitude and perspective—whether our focus is on the physical or the spiritual. If we, as an aging demographic, put as much emphasis on gaining knowledge, maturity, and wisdom as we do on eliminating wrinkles, flab, and aching joints, we'd all have a better perspective on aging.

For me, spiritual growth has made getting older an experience to savor. I'm not happy a torn meniscus will prevent me from running another marathon. I'm not thrilled when my massage therapist tells me I have knots on my knots. And thank goodness I never have to fit into my old naval officer uniforms again. But I can still swim a mile in a half hour, I can still perform an hour-long concert without having to sit down, and I can still consume solid food without drooling. So for the time being, age has not gotten the better of me physically, and

I intend to use the strength I'm given during every year I have left to do good and serve God.

Where is all this leading? Despite getting older, I have more contentment at this point in life than I've ever had. Why? Because I've learned some important lessons in Christian living over the years, and they have given me an unshakable reliance on God's provision, assurance of my eternal destiny, and a desire to do more of what he wants me to do. The only problem is that I wish I'd known some of these things when I was younger. It would have made the journey to this somewhat advanced age a little more fulfilling.

So who is the intended audience of this book? Everyone who can read because all of us were once younger, and we will inevitably get older. It's never too early or late to learn these important life lessons. Are there more than ten? Of course, but that would make for too long a book. And if you're like me, you want nuggets in your books, a big return on your reading time investment. If you're quick, this is a one or two session read, but my prayer is that you'll want to revisit the book every now and then. I've had an amazing and blessed life. But rather than a normal memoir, I want my written legacy to be an encouragement to believers and, for those still searching for meaning in life, an irresistible pull to the Savior of mankind, Jesus Christ.

There were a few criteria I laid out for myself in writing this book, criteria I look for in books that I select to read. First, it had to be relatively short, to keep my writing and your reading manageable. I have never read *War and Peace* nor do I intend to, no matter how great a novel it is. It's too long for my attention span, and in this age of digital communications, thirty-second ads, and instant information availability, I'm sure many share my short attention span. Second, it had to be compartmentalized, subdivided into sections easily read in a few minutes. Third, it had to be understandable by anyone capable of reading plain English. I have picked up and subsequently put down books that required a dictionary close at hand. A dictionary is definitely not needed for this read. Fourth and finally, it had to be worth writing. I will let you, the reader, be the judge of that.

For those who like a book that flows, with successive sections building on one another, you will be partially rewarded. There is some continuity of lessons, but each stands on its own as well. I pray that these lessons learned are informative and interesting reading, but that they also inspire and motivate. Enjoy!

ACKNOWLEDGMENTS

I have learned through my years of military service and business how important it is to obtain unbiased opinions about what you write. In my consulting work, my partner and I review each other's emails before we send them out. This practice has saved us from embarrassment or worse on many occasions.

How much more important it is to have your creative writing evaluated before the digital equivalent of putting your pencil down. I do this with all my song albums and have done it again with this book. And so I thank Pamela Smith-Vos, Sherry Faddoul, and Brad Elliott, who have read and commented on the content of this work in its draft stage.

As you read this book, you may, on occasion, think you have read or heard about a particular topic before. You're probably right. I am merely a conduit of knowledge I've picked up over my lifetime and fully admit that most of what I discuss herein is not original thinking. As Ecclesiastes 1:9 reminds us, "...there is nothing new under the sun." I have read books or seen videos on much of the subject matter and wish I could remember all the sources, so I could give proper credit. Alas, I cannot, so let me list those I can remember and thank them for providing the insightful material for this writing.

- First and foremost, thank you, Lord, for your inspired Word, which provides the foundation for this book's content.
- Thank you to the explorers in the field of lesson 10, including Eric Hovind, Kent Hovind, Ken Ham, Paul Taylor, Ray Comfort, and their associated organizations.
- Thank you to Erick Elkins, who prompted me to think critically about the earth history I had been exposed to all my life and, until his intervention, had accepted without question.
- Thank you to my many pastors, mentors, and Christian leaders over the years and their excellent teaching, which has been such an important part of my growth. These wonderful people of faith include Dave Ward, Ron Ward, Tim Dubeau, John Elder, Steve Zahare, John Guillott, and Ron Hood. I could not have written this book without sharing in your friendship and knowledge.

LESSON 1

Proof of God Shouldn't Be Necessary, But It's Out There

The Urban Dictionary says that "blind faith occurs when someone puts their faith into something without any evidence." This may be a perfectly adequate term in the secular realm, but for multiple reasons, the phrase shouldn't even exist in a spiritual context.

Not everyone "knows" God, but believe it or not, everyone knows that God exists. Romans 1:20 says, "For since the creation of the world God's invisible qualities—his eternal power and divine nature—have been clearly seen, being understood from what has been made, so that people are without excuse." What are the alternatives with respect to God? We can do either of the following:

- Know and reject,

- Know and ignore,
- Know and tolerate,
- Know and hate, or
- Know and accept & follow.

Not knowing isn't anywhere on the list. If the Bible is trustworthy—and this book devotes considerable energy to showing this is the case—there is no such thing as an atheist, just a willful rejecter of God.

God's Word alone should be sufficient to bring everyone to him. Romans 10:17 says, "So then faith comes by hearing, and hearing by the Word of God" (NKJV). I pray every reader follows this guidance and that of Jeremiah 29:13: "You will seek me and find me when you seek me with all your heart." But for those who won't listen to God's Word or the "you just have to believe" argument some Christians pose, I can somewhat relate to your point of view. During my Christian baby steps, I wasn't 100 percent convinced my beliefs were grounded. Doubts would creep into my brain. What if my belief in God was just wishful thinking?

Human minds are naturally wired to want proof prior to believing anything. It's the scientific method. We carry it over to the spiritual realm: "I'll believe in God if he proves he exists." I contend that he has, but if your idea of proof is some sort of unambiguous visible or audible sign from above, it just doesn't work that way. When the Pharisees asked Jesus for a sign, he answered, "A wicked and adulterous generation asks for a miraculous sign!" (Matt. 12:39a). After all the miracles Jesus had performed, these hypocrites had the audacity to ask for more proof.

I view the argument of doubters today in the same way. After all God has done to demonstrate his existence through creation and history, people still want more proof. An attitude that demands miraculous signs as a condition for belief does not please God. As Jesus said to Thomas, "Because you have seen me, you have believed; blessed are those who have not seen and yet have believed" (John 20:29).

Like me, most true believers soon see their doubts about God's existence disappear, and their assurance becomes unshakable. However, for the skeptic, the fence walker, and the tentative believer who are still having doubts, the remainder of this lesson presents some evidences that, in my opinion, indisputably establish the existence of our amazing and wonderful God.

Before I share, however, let me be blunt. An awesome and all-powerful God is in control of a reality beyond the confines of this universe. This awesome God loves you, wants you to be a part of that reality, and has provided a clear path for it to happen. But this awesome God is also just, and this should cause fear and trepidation in the heart of the nonbeliever. So if you are someone who still feels the need for proof, please consider the evidence carefully.

Just Look at the Universe

Would anyone look at the intricacies of a high performance automobile engine or a mechanical watch movement and believe that the parts came into existence by themselves and then miraculously came together to form precision mechanisms? This would, of course, be a silly proposition. Everyone knows that there is a designer and builder behind such machines.

Yet so many are willing to accept that billions of years ago, nothing exploded into something, from which all the material in the universe came into existence and resulted in the remarkable order of the stars, planets, and galaxies. Then, over eons of time, life evolved from chemicals to simple molecules to the complex animals that exist on the earth today, among them human beings.

But you say science proves the big bang theory and evolution, correct? Not even close. By definition, scientific processes are observable and testable. Therefore, science can neither prove or disprove something that happened when no human being was around. Science, however, can provide insight into the origin of the universe, and I believe it is clearly on the side of how the Bible said it happened.

The notion that the universe came into existence and operates through natural processes alone contradicts inviolate laws of physics, including the first and second laws of thermodynamics, which all life and non-life processes obey. There is a lot of excellent writing on this subject, but in rather simplistic terms, here is my take:

- The First Law of Thermodynamics is one of conservation and says that the substance of the universe—matter and energy—is a constant and cannot be created or destroyed. So if some fourteen billion years ago, the universe originated from the big bang—the explosion of a very dense cosmic egg into which all the substance of the universe was compressed—where did the initial material in this primordial egg come from? A key connected question is this: Time-wise, what came before this event? Every secular and supposed scientific viewpoint on the origin of the universe is flawed. The only answer that makes any sense in terms of this law is that someone outside the physical universe and outside of our timeline must have created it.

- The Second Law of Thermodynamics says that disorder or entropy in the universe is always increasing. I clean my house periodically, but it always gets dirty again. My clothes fade and wear out. Things periodically need repair and paint. My car breaks down now and then. Death and decay of every living thing are inevitable. Left to itself, nothing becomes more complex. Simply put, the trend in the real world is always downhill, not uphill. Yet naturalistic theories about processes in the universe, including biological evolution, propose that atoms and molecules ordered themselves into increasingly complex and beneficial arrangements in complete conflict with this law. The development of order from chaos in both physical and biological realms is scientifically impossible.

I will return to the subject of creation later in this lesson and in lesson 10. However, for this discussion, let me conclude with my conviction that the universe and its contents, the laws that govern its operation, and the life within it were created by an amazing designer who continues to sustain it and maintain its order. The next time you view a solar eclipse and see our moon and sun perfectly aligned in this awe-inspiring astronomical display, don't try to convince yourself this is a happenstance of nature. It's just one of countless examples of God's amazing creative power that should astound us and draw us to him.

Just Look at Earth

There is a great video I own called *The Privileged Planet*. While it is not an overtly Christian film, it explains the rare and intricate combination of factors that makes the earth suitable not only for complex life, but for exploration of and scientific discovery about the universe. Though reference to God is infrequent and tangential, it is impossible to reach the end of the movie and conclude that there is no intelligent designer at work within the cosmos. You are also left with the impression that our planet is alone in its unique privilege of being hospitable to life.

I enjoyed the movie, *ET*, when it came out in 1982 and continue to enjoy the *Star Trek* series of shows and movies, as well as other movies about space exploration and alien life forms. But I can get entertainment value from these fantasies while, at the same time, recognizing the implausibility of the story lines. The search for extra-terrestrial intelligence (SETI) movement continues with a passion, but I am convinced that no concrete evidence of sentient life beyond our planet will ever be found.

Why do I believe this? Because as *The Privileged Planet* film implies, God created the earth for life, and he created everything else for his glory and for our appreciation of his awesome power.

We'll talk about the "Goldilocks zone" in regard to life contentment later on, but let's take a moment and look at this term with regard to the earth's capability to sustain life and make it interesting.

Earth is perfect in size, and its gravity holds close to the surface the unique nitrogen-oxygen atmosphere required for life. If it were smaller like Mercury or larger like Jupiter, an atmosphere would be impossible. Earth is the perfect distance from the sun, not too hot and not too cold, just like Goldilocks' preferred porridge temperature. Of course, the right temperature prevents us from either freezing or burning up and ensures the water essential for life remains a liquid in most regions. What is truly amazing about this phenomenon is how little a variation in distance from the sun would be required to completely throw off this delicate temperature balance.

Correspondingly, the moon is the perfect size and distance from the earth, with a revolution time and gravitational pull that optimally balance tidal patterns to keep the oceans from stagnation, yet prevent them from flooding the continents.

Also, the earth's distance from the sun and our solar system's position within the Milky Way facilitate an amazing view of the heavens unimpaired by too much sunlight, dense star clusters, or galactic dust.

Many presume that with countless billions of stars out there, there are surely other worlds with life like ours. However, there is another side to the equation: the probability that all of the physical and chemical factors required to support complex life are present simultaneously on one of these worlds. The list of these factors continues to grow, but conservatively assuming twenty factors and a one-in-ten chance that a factor is present, the probability that another planet as habitable as the earth exists is roughly 10^{-15}, or a thousandth of a trillionth, for every hundred billion star systems, an infinitesimally small number that perhaps suggests our earth could be unique in the universe. Math aside, I contend that life on Earth alone is exactly how God planned it.

And just how would Christianity fit into the idea of other inhabited worlds? Romans 6:10 says, "The death he [Jesus] died, he died to sin once for all." If there were countless life-supporting planets and who knows how many intelligent ETs out there, wouldn't Jesus have had to go there and die for them as well? Yes, he would have; but of course, he didn't. God's plan for life has a single point of focus, and that is Earth, where his eternal aims have been executed throughout history and continue to unfold.

Earth is truly a one-of-a-kind planet. One of a kind will rarely win you a poker hand, but it wonderfully describes God's intention for the planet that we humans share with the enormous variety of incredible animals and plants. What a remarkable creation.

Here is a depiction of the cross of Christ overlaying the earth from one of my early albums. His protective and caring shadow surely covers the world.

Just Look at Israel

Most people don't believe in modern day miracles, but the existence of the nation of Israel to this day is a testimony to God's existence. Deuteronomy 4:34 says, "Has any god ever tried to take for himself one nation out of another nation, by testings, by signs and wonders, by war, by a mighty hand and an outstretched arm, or by great and awesome deeds, like all the things the Lord your God did for you in Egypt before your very eyes?"

These words were spoken to the Israelites—not to the Hittites, the Edomites, the Amorites, the Jebusites, or any of the other "ites" that coexisted with Israel during Old Testament days. Not a one of those people groups exists today as a nation, only God's chosen people. Every single prophesy about Israel has been or is being fulfilled, including the regathering of its people as a nation, just like the Bible says:

> "I will bring you from the nations and gather you from the countries where you have been scattered—with a mighty hand and an outstretched arm and with outpoured wrath" (Ezek. 20:34).

> "In that day the Lord will reach out his hand a second time to reclaim the remnant that is left of his people from Assyria, from Lower Egypt, from Upper Egypt, from Cush,

> from Elam, from Babylonia, from
> Hamath, and from the islands of the
> sea. He will raise a banner for the
> nations and gather the exiles of Israel;
> he will assemble the scattered people
> of Judah from the four quarters of
> the earth" (Isa. 11:11–12).

No other group of people in history has been dispersed around the world for 2,500 years, then, against all odds, returned to its homeland and re-established itself as a nation. It has happened once, and it will not happen again. And we can be sure that prophesies about the future of Israel will be fulfilled as well. If you want miraculous proof of God, I give you the nation of Israel.

Just Look at You

A book I love reading again and again is called *In Six Days* and is subtitled *Why Fifty Scientists Choose to Believe in Creation*. All of these scientists have PhD degrees in their fields of specialty, which include biology, chemistry, and genetics. All of them have chosen to believe in a six-day creation over Darwinian evolution or any compromise position such as theistic evolution or progressive creation. By six days, these scientists mean literal twenty-four-hour days, not days that represent long periods of time to accommodate the evolutionary process. Their contention is supported by the most reliable Bible interpreters, who conclude that in the context of

Genesis 1, the Hebrew work *yom* (day) can only mean a twenty-four-hour time period.

One of the common focal points of the essays in this book is the sheer impossibility of evolution explaining the immense complexity of life, even at the single-cell level. The forming of a complex living organism by chance without intelligent input has never been, nor ever will be, demonstrated. Even staunch supporters of evolution see the theory only as a mechanism of life progression, not of life origin.

When decoding of the human DNA molecule began decades ago, scientists discovered a unique internal language composed of billions of genetic letters—stored information that gives instructions for building proteins, the building blocks of all life. As hard as it is to conceive, the human DNA molecule contains the detailed information equivalent to books occupying nearly fifty feet of library shelves. This is a bit easier to imagine when you consider the digital storage capacity of today, but still a phenomenal amount of information in a tiny space.

Scientists say that a teaspoon of DNA could contain the information needed to build all the proteins for every species that has lived on the earth. I do not believe, for one second, that evolution could miniaturize and sequence all this information into the genetic instruction manual required for life to exist. There is a superior intelligence behind such a system.

We could go on to discuss the remarkable processing capacity of the brain and its ability to simultaneously produce reasoning, relationships, feelings, and plans. We could talk about how the eye can distinguish color, focus, and handle millions of visual messages. In his *The Origin of Species*, Darwin himself said, "If it could be demonstrated that any complex organ existed which could not possibly have been formed by numerous, successive, slight modifications, my theory would absolutely break down." Organs such as the brain and the eye are "irreducibly complex." Like even the simplest mechanical systems (for example, the mousetrap), all the components of these organs have to be there from the start in order for them to work.

Beyond complexity, we could talk about the need for the interdependency of parts (for example, muscle, nerve, and brain) to create functionality within our bodies. Even if evolution could explain how these components of our anatomy improved over time, which it cannot, it could never explain where they came from in the first place.

Perhaps Edwin Conklin said it best in the January 1963 *Reader's Digest*: "The probability of life originating from accident is comparable to the probability of the unabridged dictionary resulting from an explosion in a print shop." If you ask me, it takes a greater degree of blind faith to believe in the "religion" of evolution than in the creation model of the Bible.

"How many are your works, Lord! In wisdom you made them all; the earth is full of your creatures" (Ps. 104:24). Surely, the mind-boggling complexity and orderliness of living things demonstrate that the earth and all that resides in it did not result from chance, random processes.

Yes, you and I are complex biological entities as are all animals, but unlike most animals, we humans can relate to the One who created us and gave us the ability to recognize these remarkable complexities of life.

Just Look at the Resurrection

At Easter services, many pastors start out the service by saying, "He is risen," and the fellowship responds, "He is risen indeed." The crucifixion and resurrection of Jesus is a well-documented historical event—not just in the Bible, but also by secular historians such as Flavius Josephus.

Sir Lionel Luckhoo (1914–1997) was a Guyana-born politician, diplomat, and lawyer who achieved fame for his 245 consecutive successful defenses in murder cases. For this feat, he is in *The Guinness Book of World Records*. Here is what Sir Luckhoo stated before his death about the resurrection of Jesus:

> "I have spent more than forty-two years as a defense trial attorney in many parts of the world and am still in active practice. I have been fortunate to secure a number of successes in jury trials, and I say unequivocally that the evidence for the resurrection of Jesus Christ is so overwhelming that it compels acceptance by proof which leaves absolutely no room for doubt."[1]

Timothy Keller (born in 1950) is an American pastor, theologian, Christian apologist, and author. He says the following:

> "If Jesus rose from the dead, then you have to accept all that he said; if he didn't rise from the dead, then why worry about any of what he said. The issue on which everything hangs is not whether or not you like his teaching, but whether or not he rose from the dead."[2]

So what if all the evidence points to this truth: Jesus was killed and rose from the dead to defy all we know about life and death? If Jesus truly is alive, he is the only leader of a major world religion who is. And if he is alive, isn't it worth considering every word he says about a relationship with the Father through him and how to live our lives?

The truth is that no one can be ambivalent about Jesus Christ. Everyone must say either yes or no because as the following lyrics for a song I wrote back in 2005 suggest, not answering is the same as saying no.

"Say Yes"

In the time it takes to bow your head
In the time it takes to pray
In the time it takes to give your heart
Your sin is washed away

In the moment that you make the choice
To begin your life anew
That's the moment that you realize
There's only one thing left to do

First Chorus
Say yes to God, say yes
To Jesus Christ, his only Son
Consider all he's done
To lift you from the depths of darkness
Say yes to life, say yes
To freedom from the chains of sin
And once you've asked him in
You'll never be the same

When he asks us if we'll follow him
We must choose the way to go
And for those who never tell him yes
It's just the same as saying no

Second Chorus
Say yes to God, say yes
To Jesus Christ, his only Son
The victory has been won
And now, the choice is up to you
Say yes to life, say yes
To freedom from the chains of sin
And once you've asked him in
You'll never be the same
No you'll never be the same

***

I mentioned at the beginning of this lesson that everyone instinctively knows God exists. I concluded with the action required to turn that knowledge of God into a relationship with God. This will be the first of several appeals within this book for readers to take that action if they have not done so already because I feel it's the most important decision anyone will make in his or her lifetime. It would simplify life if we could all disregard or hand off this responsibility, but we cannot. And this leads us to lesson 2.

LESSON 2

God Only Has Children, No Grandchildren

I admit I took the above title from a pastor's awesome sermon, but it so accurately describes a truth that I think many misunderstand, I had to use it. Another way to say this is that there are only first-generation Christians.

We can come from a Christian family, we can be a participant in infant baptism, we can go to church all our lives, we can serve noble causes, we can memorize scripture verses, and we can know every Bible story by heart. But none of these establishes our personal relationship with Jesus Christ, "the way, the truth, and the life" (John 14:6) and God's provision for the redemption of humankind. If we are so fortunate as to have Christian parents, they cannot wish us into a right relationship with Jesus. Each of us is required to embark on that journey of acceptance and belief as an individual, and once we reach the age of accountability, we all need to make a decision.

I'll share my unique journey, but let me begin by saying that each journey is prompted by a deep spiritual need that resides in all of us.

A God-Shaped Hole

We all have God-shaped holes in our hearts that only he can fill. This is one reason why there is so much malcontent in the United States today. On mission trips to Honduras, Ecuador, Costa Rica, and Mexico, I have met adults and children who materially have next to nothing. Yet there is great joy and hope within because they have the Lord in their hearts in the here and now and live for the hope of an eternity with their Savior. On the other hand, I know many people here in the USA who have every possession one can own, yet they are miserable. Why? It's because possessions cannot fill that God-shaped hole. It took a long time for me to learn this lesson. I first learned it in my late teens. I've had to relearn it over and over, and I wish I would have learned it for good when I was younger. As these lyrics from my 2006 album, *24 Hours*, explain, God created us with a spiritual component that only his Spirit can fill.

"Spirit Needs Spirit"

All of us have a need
The world cannot fulfill
We try to prove it wrong
But never will
'Cause there's a part of us

Beyond the flesh and soul
Just one thing fits that space
And makes us whole

Chorus
Spirit needs Spirit
Like the night needs day
Nothing else will ever
Chase the dark away
Spirit needs Spirit
Like the earth needs rain
And when his Spirit fills us
We'll never thirst again

It's easy to believe
The treasures we hold dear
Can bring us happiness
But one thing's clear
If all our hearts' desires
Tomorrow come to pass
We'll still be missing out
On joy that lasts

Bridge
And when you hear this song
I hope you realize
When you're feeling empty
Only Spirit satisfies

My Awakening

I had basically good parents. We were not rich, but I never wanted for anything. I never recall missing a meal, and Christmases and birthdays always included some great gifts. My father, in particular, saw to it that I participated in activities such as Little League and Boy Scouts, which helped me grow physically and as a decent, well-rounded young man.

My parents took me to church on Sundays and taught me right from wrong. I listened to sermon after sermon in the various Presbyterian churches we attended in the Philadelphia area, and I knew about all the great men and women in the Bible from stories in Sunday school. I knew about Jesus, but I didn't know Jesus because no one had ever clearly explained the Gospel message to me.

Isn't it amazing that you can know the whole life story of Jesus yet never know how that story relates to you on a personal level? So when I went off to the U.S. Naval Academy at the age of seventeen, the God-shaped hole in my heart was still unfilled.

Very few events at or around the Naval Academy were voluntary. They were either mandatory or prohibited. So when an optional evening of musical entertainment was offered as an alternative to studying in my room, I jumped at the opportunity. I was somewhat dismayed when it turned out to be a "religious" singing group (I can't even remember the group's name), but I stayed because it was preferable to studying. Then, at the end of the show, for the first time in my life, I heard the Gospel of Jesus Christ clearly explained.

Wait a minute! I had gone to church my whole life and was even now singing in the Academy Protestant choir every Sunday. My family had celebrated the Christian holidays of Christmas and Easter, both about Jesus, although Santa Claus and the Easter Bunny seemed to get more attention at the time. I understood that Jesus was miraculously born to a virgin named Mary; that he taught, prophesied, and healed; and that, as a young man, he was killed on a cross and rose again. I knew all these things. What I didn't know was that he did all that for me personally!

Now in an auditorium at the Naval Academy on an evening when my primary motivation was to get out of studying, I was learning that Jesus lived, died, and rose again for me as an individual, as well as for the rest of humanity. The message was so simple yet so profound. So much clarity and understanding would follow in the years to come, but at that moment, I said yes to Jesus; and my life as a true Christian began.

Even though I would have liked to have had this experience earlier in life, I believe—age-wise—I still had it well before my parents. My father, a church-goer his whole life and an elder in the Presbyterian church, accepted the Lord only a few years before his passing in 1979 and became an on-fire witness. I'm not sure when my mother accepted Jesus, but when I talked with her shortly before her death in 2005, she assured me that she knew him and knew where she was going.

A Street Sweeper in Heaven

I admit that the fruit of my early Christian walk was pretty meager. I didn't want to give up all the things that, in my naivety, I thought brought pleasure. I was a navy guy, and the pressure to conform to the wayward lifestyle was tremendous. My commitment was superficial, which reminds me of another person's early walk.

My best friend for many years was a guy I served with in submarines and with whom I worked for two decades after we both left submarine active duty. He knew I was a Christian, but for a long time, my witness fell on deaf ears. Then one day, with the flip of a switch, the light went on; and he became a believer. The problem was he had a hard time leaving his old sinful ways behind, and the evidence of his conversion wasn't easy to find during those first few years after he accepted the Lord.

When we would talk about it, he would say that he understood he wasn't living the Christian life. He was hoping to get better; but if he should die before he put his old ways behind him, at least he would be a street sweeper in heaven, which was far better than any job in that other place.

Now, I'm fairly sure the streets of heaven won't ever need sweeping, but this is a comment worth a bit more discussion. Before that, though, let me say that my friend ultimately did put his sinful ways behind him and went on to become a full-time missionary. He's with the Lord in heaven now, and believe me, he's no street sweeper.

If for No Other Reason, Isn't It Worth Playing It Safe?

When I started reading the Bible with more focus, one of the stories that told me that I had escaped a horrifying eternity was the one in Luke 16:19–31, which tells about a rich man and a beggar named Lazarus (not the same Lazarus, by the way, that Jesus raised from the dead). Verses 22–24 say:

> "The time came when the beggar died and the angels carried him to Abraham's side. The rich man also died and was buried. In Hades, where he was in torment, he looked up and saw Abraham far away, with Lazarus by his side. So he called to him, 'Father Abraham, have pity on me and send Lazarus to dip the tip of his finger in water and cool my tongue, because I am in agony in this fire.' "

The story goes on to explain the uncrossable chasm between these two post-life destinations and to further contrast the comfort of one versus the torment of the other. Perhaps the most disturbing part of this story is that the two destinations appear to be within sight of one another. I'm not sure if it's true, but can you imagine the horror and dismay of seeing heaven from hell and knowing you can never cross over?

I think my friend was onto something with his street sweeper comment. After coming to Christ, if we are weak followers for the rest of our lives and end up with few of the promised rewards of obedience and service, we will at least avoid the punishment of rejecting God's offer of salvation through Jesus. At least we will not end up for all eternity in a place prepared not for human beings, but for Satan and other fallen angels. If it does nothing else, maybe the fear of this eternity should motivate everyone to consider the claim of Christ: "I am the way and the truth and the life. No one comes to the Father except through me" (John 14:6).

You may say, "I'm not into religion." Well I'm not into religion either. Religion is thinking our own merit or works can somehow reach a God unreachable by human effort. Christianity, on the other hand, is accepting that God reached out to us through his Son. It's about relationship, not religion. No 'religion' can claim that its leader is still alive. Mohammed, dead; Joseph Smith, dead; Buddha and Krishna—if they even existed as humans—dead. However, Jesus lives and continues to intercede on our behalf.

If you're not convinced, here's a question: What if what the Bible says about the reality of heaven and hell is true? I hope everyone comes to Christ because they want a relationship with their Maker and want to grow in knowing and serving him. But if not for those reasons, wouldn't you want to play it safe? At least you'll be a "street sweeper" in the good place.

And here's my confession. Playing it safe was a consideration when I first believed. I knew, for a fact, I didn't want to end up where the rich man in the above story was. Now, I can assure you that God won't leave you with that shallowness of faith for very long. Jesus said he came to give life abundantly, and that's what he will do if you let him.

Remember that God doesn't want anyone to perish (2 Pet. 3:9) and neither do I. But to reiterate the crux of this lesson learned, every believer is a first-generation believer. Your parents or grandparents can't pray you into the kingdom. It's your choice and yours alone. If you get only one thing out of this book, this is the message. Say yes to Jesus as Savior and avoid the consequences of saying no. Once you do, your life will change in so many ways, and you'll wonder how you ever lived without him.

Here are lyrics that summarize this lesson. We have a God-shaped hole that requires filling, and Jesus is the one who can do just that.

"Only Jesus Satisfies"

You can put your faith in fame and fortune
Search for power and riches high and low
Reach the end of every human longing
And not discover what believers know
All worldly gain, all earthly belongings
Never really make you whole
There's only one thing on earth or in heaven
That can fill the empty soul

Chorus
You can keep all your prized possessions
There's no joy in what our money buys
Hear the wisdom now, heed the lesson
Only Jesus satisfies

He gives purpose, he gives meaning
He will show what real life holds in store
When he fills you with his presence
All you'll want and need is more and more
Everything else that you've ever lived for
Is only effort made in vain
With him in your life, there's nothing to lose
No, and everything to gain

***

To wrap up, back in my late teens, I exercised faith,
right? Not so fast. If you reread these first two lessons, you'll
realize I haven't said anything about exercising or demon-
strating faith. Why is that? Let's move on to lesson 3.

LESSON 3

I Am Not in Control of My Own Faith

I believed, I confessed, I accepted. Those are actions I can take. But I have learned that true biblical faith—not the mere expression of *faith* as a commitment of belief—is not mine to exercise; it comes from God. Perhaps, in the secular sense, one can demonstrate faith—some of it blind faith. When we sit in a chair, we have faith that it will hold us up because of the evidence: a sitting surface connected to four unbroken legs reaching the floor. The words *faith* and *confidence* can be used interchangeably.

But let's look at some of what the Bible says about Christian faith:

- It is the gift of God (Eph. 2:8).
- It is the reality of what we hope for and the proof of what we don't see (Heb. 11:1).

- Jesus is the author and perfecter of faith (Heb. 12:2).
- God has allotted to each a measure of faith (Rom. 12:3).

None of these verses implies that any of us has total control over our faith. God has given some amount of faith to me, and the Bible says he gives a certain amount of faith to all believers. Let's break down what the Bible says about faith and what I have learned through my experiences.

Faith Comes from God

"For it is by grace you have been saved, through faith—and this is not from yourselves, it is the gift of God" (Eph. 2:8). In this verse, what is it that comes from God: grace, salvation, faith? In my opinion, all of them come from God.

Hebrews 11:1 gives us more insight into what faith really is: "Now faith is confidence in what we hope for and assurance about what we do not see." This verse tells us that faith is much more than just believing in something. When I started my Christian walk in my late teens, I thought faith was a point event, a narrowly defined leap from unbelief to belief in God and his provision for my salvation. Over time, I've learned that faith has substance and quantity. It is a long-term proposition and by no means a constant. It is a conviction I have about spiritual things that allows me to think and act as if they were assured of happening. And all this does not come from within.

Let's look at one example—eternal life. "I write these things to you who believe in the name of the Son of God so that you may know that you have eternal life" (1 John 5:13). Notice the word *know* in this verse—not hope or assume. It's a certainty. I am as confident that I will live forever in a place the Lord has prepared for me as I am that I will take my next breath—in fact, more so, because none of us is guaranteed the latter.

I mentioned that faith is not a constant. This is true, and unfortunately, it is my experience that faith does not always seem like it is on the rise and growing. Every now and then, even to this day, I feel my faith being tested, especially when I'm sick, struggling, stressed, afraid, lonely, or feeling abandoned. What I have learned, however, is that this is an irrational feeling. It is allowing an internal perception of things to influence an external provision. Just this realization is a faith-strengthening factor.

As God increases our measure of faith, the results are amazing. We have greater joy and peace (Rom. 15:13), more love for others (1 John 4:7), power over Satan's attacks (Eph. 6:16), and greater obedience (Heb. 11:8).

Faith Comes from Hearing about Jesus

So faith comes from God, but how does it come from God? To reiterate a verse from lesson 1 using the NIV translation, Romans 10:17 says, "Consequently, faith comes from hearing the message, and the message is heard through the Word about Christ."

Faith comes from hearing about Jesus through the Word. In my earlier walk, some of my doubts arose from my perception that God was distant and disconnected from individual lives in this day and age. After all, in the Old Testament, he verbally stopped Abraham from sacrificing his son in the nick of time, he wrestled with Jacob, he talked to Moses through a burning bush, he manifested himself as a pillar of cloud or fire, and he spoke to his nation through thousands of years of prophets. Why was God so silent today?

I contend that God is not as silent as we might think, but the reason that there is not as much overt and direct contact as there was during Old Testament days is that we have at our disposal something those in the BC era did not: his Word, specifically the New Testament that speaks about his divine purposes accomplished through his Son, Jesus Christ.

It is when we hear about Jesus from God's Word and respond through the ABCs of becoming a Christian—*A*dmit we are sinners, *B*elieve Jesus paid the penalty for that sin, and *C*onfess Jesus as Savior and Lord—we are granted the gift of faith.

I believe the faith granted at this moment is our initial measure from Jesus the author of our faith—an imperfect faith because if you recall from Hebrews 12:2, Jesus is also the perfecter of our faith. And if something is capable of being perfected, it must start out an imperfect thing.

Initial Faith Is Instantaneous; Perfect Faith Takes a Lifetime or More

A simple prayer is all it takes to accept Jesus as Lord; to be forgiven of all sin past, present, and future; and to know, for certain, your eternal destination. You can pause your reading and pray this prayer right now if you are moved to do so.

We are justified by this initial faith—"just as if" we never sinned. What an amazing sense of freedom. Sins are forgiven, but more than forgiven, they are forever forgotten. "As far as the east is from the west, so far has he removed our transgressions from us" (Ps. 103:12). Why is it east and west and not north and south? It's because east and west truly never meet. You can head east forever and never be heading west. On the other hand, north and south meet at the two poles. Go far enough north or south, and you ultimately go the other direction. Here are the words of one of the first Christian songs I ever wrote, a song that speaks of God's disposition of the believer's sin.

"Forgiven, Forgotten, Forever"

When Jesus of Nazareth lived on the earth
He spoke of God's plan to forgive
The sins of humanity present and past
And those of a world yet to live
Even his faithful could not understand
But he knew that the blood he must spill
Would once and for all lay the sins of mankind
At the foot of a cross on a hill

Chorus
God sent us Jesus, the last sacred lamb
To lay down his life for the burden of man
Gone were my sins when he died on that tree
Forgiven, forgotten, forever they'll be

But more than forgiven, the follower's sin
Is never again to be seen
For God said as far as the east is from west
Still farther your sins are from me
And so in his mercy we find higher ground
And freedom from fearing a fall
For the Lord in his holiness cannot condemn
What he's promised he'll never recall

After this initial faith comes the lifetime pursuit of
living for God, the perfection of our faith through Jesus,
also called sanctification. It's not easy, it's not overnight,
and no one reaches the final destination in this lifetime.
On the day we all breathe our last on this earth, the sanctification process is still ongoing.

***

To conclude this lesson, I believe God's Word is
clear about faith. It is his gift to all believers. It is having
absolute certainty about the spiritual realities of life in
the here and now and the hereafter. It is the internal fuel
that motivates us to live for God and serve his kingdom.

Perhaps we have some limited control over our faith
if God's faith allotment is in any way proportional to our

trust and dependence on him and the commitment of our walk with him. But I see no biblical support of the notion that faith is something we develop from within. God allots faith according to his divine will. I don't know what metrics he uses or why, but I trust that I have the measure I need to accomplish what he wants me to accomplish.

Once, a person told me he had lost his faith. I asked if he had trusted in Jesus as his Savior. He said yes but that he had backslidden terribly. I told him that, perhaps, his faith was weaker but that he could not lose his initial measure of faith because it didn't come from him in the first place and that if his trust in Christ was sincere, his salvation was secure. That's the wonder of God's gift of faith. He will never take away your initial measure. No matter how far you backslide, you always hit a comfortable stop at the nadir of saving faith.

Of course, believers should aspire to greater faith because faith is the foundation upon which the fulfilling Christian life is built. What are the products of this kind of faith? In my experience, faith products have included a clear understanding of right and wrong, contentment with whatever life brings, a desire to demonstrate our salvation through kingdom work, a closer relationship with the Lord, and a confidence in his timeless and perfect Word.

All this—what radio broadcaster Paul Harvey used to call "the rest of the story"—is the subject matter for the remaining lessons in this book.

There Are Some Things God Really Hates

Over the years, I have realized that one essential product of faith is insightful discernment between right and wrong, resulting in a greater obedience to God's commands and a desire to influence others toward such obedience.

The past three-quarters of a century have been a time of supposed enlightenment, during which the black and white of right and wrong have been replaced by infinite shades of gray. As part of the so-called evolution of consciousness within society, people have erased the word *sin* from their vocabulary as archaic and irrelevant to modern living.

But the Bible tells a very different story. Like it or not, sin is a core part of our being. When I hear anyone say that human beings are basically good with a bad streak, I smile inside. By my observation, it's the exact opposite, and only by the indwelling of the Holy Spirit and the measure of faith God provides does the good emerge from our sinful existences.

The Disease with Which We Are Born

Every one of us has an inborn sinful nature—an unfortunate inheritance from our ancient ancestors, Adam and Eve, and their joint disobedience of God's command in the Garden of Eden. Everyone since has lived with the consequence of that action.

Who teaches two-year-old children to throw tantrums when they don't get their way? Who teaches them to snatch someone else's possession as if it were their own, then lie in order to avoid the consequences of their action? Who teaches kids to blame others when they know they are at fault? The answer is no one. It's part of original sin, for which there is only one remedy.

As these kids grow older, observation of their parents, suggestive media, or other influences might prompt more serious sinful actions such as bullying of other kids, stealing or shoplifting, or even taking a life; but these are still manifestations of a nature with which we are born—perhaps exacerbated by family, friends, and environment.

God's Hate List

The Bible is clear on the things that God detests. Obviously, the Ten Commandments is a good starting point. We can also look in the book of Proverbs, specifically chapter 6, verses 16–19, to understand some of the attitudes and actions that God hates. In fact, we are told that some things are an abomination to God.

> "There are six things the Lord hates, seven that are detestable to him: haughty eyes, a lying tongue, hands that shed innocent blood, a heart that devises wicked schemes, feet that are quick to rush into evil, a false witness who pours out lies, and a person who stirs up conflict in the community" (Prov. 6:16–19, ESV).

Your initial thought might be that you do not have haughty eyes, your lies are usually white ones, you've never murdered anyone, and bearing false witness and sowing discord are not your thing. It's time to ask a few questions.

- Did you ever roll your eyes or give a contemptuous look in response to something said to you? If so, you have haughty eyes.
- Did you ever extend flattery to gain something from someone? If so, you have a lying tongue.
- Did you ever abuse an animal for amusement? If so, you have shed innocent blood.
- Did you ever plot to deceive, hurt, or get revenge on someone? If so, you have a heart that devises wicked schemes.

- Did you ever join in doing wrong when authority was not present? If so, you have feet that are quick to rush into evil.
- Did you ever cover for someone who did something wrong? If so, you are a false witness who pours out lies.
- Did you ever initiate or share one word of gossip? If so, you are a person who stirs up conflict in the community.

Have you ever done any one of these? If so, your life is not sin free.

The bottom line is that God hates all sin, and there are no shades of gray as society would like you to believe. Sin is sin, and God's standard for perfection is no sin at all. No one other than the Son of God has ever succeeded in following each of the Ten Commandments to the letter of the law for an entire lifetime. One lie, one covetous glance, one hurtful word—the verdict is guilty.

Shades of Gray or Black and White

In a papal letter on love and marriage, Pope Francis said the Catholic church should welcome those who are in "irregular" marriages, among them gay marriages. He was essentially telling the clergy that human life is too complicated to apply black-and-white rules.[3]

Yes, we should love and welcome everyone and never harm anyone because of their practices. And of course, everyone deserves equal protection under the laws of the

land. But I respectfully disagree with the Pope's asser-
tion that this issue is not black and white. Sin is black
and white. Political correctness has spiraled so far out of
control that we are reluctant to recognize sin for what it
is. Gay or lesbian behavior is not a lifestyle option; it is
perversion. Aborting unborn babies is not a choice; it is
murder.

But believe me when I say, with all sincerity, that I
am no less guilty than those participating in these practices. We are all sinful and therefore guilty—from the
child who tells a white lie to the serial killer.

The Remedy for Sin Is Not within Our Power

I am reminded of the story of two men trying to
jump to Santa Catalina Island from a coastal pier near
Los Angeles. With a running start, the first man jumps
an impressive fifteen feet off the end of the pier and lands
in the water. The second man, with an even longer and
faster run, catches the end of the pier perfectly and soars
twenty feet before hitting the water. As the two climb
out of the Pacific Ocean, the second man boasts of his
superior jump.

Gentlemen, both of your leaps are nearly twenty
miles from the island to which you were attempting to
jump—seriously? This humorous story illustrates the
futility of attempts to reach God by our own efforts. One
sin, no matter how small, in the midst of a life of good
deeds and serving others limits us to that twenty-foot
jump when the goal is to span the twenty-mile gap
between the pier and Catalina Island. Fortunately, the

gap between God and us has been spanned by God himself through the sacrifice of Jesus on the cross of Calvary. We all need to accept the message of the one true Gospel, that accepting Christ's sacrifice for sin is the only way to the Father.

The Problem with Gospel Alternatives

Most people say they believe in God and heaven. Of those who do, many still think they can be good enough to get to heaven based on their own efforts—the so-called works-based gospel—like the two jumpers above. For those with this belief, tell me where you draw the line on good deeds.

Wouldn't you hate to get to heaven's door and find you were one good deed short? "I'm so sorry, the threshold was 1,246 good deeds, and you were just under that number. Let me call you a taxi to your real eternal destination, and you might want to shed those outer layers of clothing."

Some people shun the Gospel because they question its fairness. What about those who have never heard? What about those who devoutly practice other religions? What about children too young to understand? What about the mentally incapacitated? I believe that our loving God has a plan for those who have not reached the point of accountability because of a young age, mental disability, or truly having never heard. "Far be it from you to do such a thing—to kill the righteous with the wicked, treating the righteous and the wicked alike. Far be it from you! Will not the Judge of all the earth do right?" (Gen. 18:25).

And with all my heart, I believe that the list of children who have not reached the point of accountability includes those in the womb who never got the chance to see the light of day, whether their physical lives ended naturally or by abortion. I had two children who began life's journey at conception and didn't make it to this world. I fully expect to see them in heaven someday.

Rather than challenging God's perfect judgment, we should all be concerned about our own eternal destinies. And for those who have heard and rejected the Gospel of salvation, the Bible is clear that there is no hope. "But wait," you say at the threshold of eternity. "I thought there would be other ways to heaven. What about the bush native?" Reply: "I've thought of and taken care of the bush native. Why weren't you more concerned about yourself?"

God's Commands Are for Our Own Good

If the above sounded more like a sermon than a lesson learned, it was all leading to these words of "Bob wisdom." There have been times in my life when I conformed to society's shades-of-gray interpretation of right and wrong and conveniently relabeled a *black* as a *shade of gray*. There have been times when I flat out knew an action was wrong and did it anyway. Every time I took either path, things did not end well. Someone invariably suffered—me, a loved one, a friend, or sometimes even a stranger.

Growing faith has given me clear discernment between right and wrong and shown me that there are always consequences in disobeying God's commands. I'm not saying that I'm now always obedient. God knows that's not true. But there is near-absolute clarity about right and wrong and instantaneous conviction when I choose unwisely.

God's rules for living are not arbitrary, and there's a reason they exist. They were written in stone in the days of Moses, they were written in the Bible as it was being penned, and they are written in our hearts today—all for our own good.

I've often asked myself why people are so negative toward God's rules for living, especially some that seem controversial in light of today's societal norms. After all, Psalm 119 celebrates God's law as perfect and life giving. I have concluded that as part of the Genesis 3 fall, along with sin and death came a perverted interpretation of God's rules for ideal living.

In the perfection of the heavenly hierarchy, the Father-Son relationship of authority and submission works perfectly as it should in the husband-wife relationship on the earth. But we have turned authority into dominance and submission into weakness, both distortions of God's model for the relationship. Worship, which should be reserved for the Holy Trinity, has been misguidedly bestowed on movie and music stars, sports heroes, politicians, and other celebrities. We have equated God's laws, which are cleansing and liberating, to secular laws, which can seem limiting and confining. Sin clouds our view of what truly is meant for our own good, believers and non-believers alike.

The Good News—Sin and Death Are Not Forever

Some twenty years ago, I listened to a guest pastor's message in the church I was attending at the time. I don't even remember the man's name, but one statement he made will be in my top ten sermon moments of all time. His Christian mother had recently died; and he recalled attending her wake, looking down at her still body, and saying out loud, "Mom, I envy you. You are now in the presence of our Savior." Talk about a comment outside of our comfort zones. Most people dread being on the other side of this life. How can death be envied? The answer is that it cannot and should not. This guest preacher was envying the life for which we were all made, not the death of this mortal shell.

This lesson has been all about what God hates; and the one thing I believe God hates, perhaps more than anything else, is death, as well as the disease and decay that lead to death. When God finished his work of creation, he said that everything was good. In Genesis 3, that all changed with our ancestors' willful disobedience, which led to spiritual death and ultimately to physical death. Death is an unfortunate artifact of the fall, a result of the sinful nature that we inherited.

The short book of Lamentations—sandwiched between Jeremiah and Ezekiel—was written by Jeremiah, the *weeping prophet*. As its name implies, the book expresses grief over the destruction of Jerusalem by the

Babylonians. Jeremiah prophesied this event, witnessed it, and, in this book, articulates his despair over it. His purpose is to teach God's people that disobedience results in suffering and sorrow.

I believe this book is a microcosm of God's ongoing lament for the earth of this dispensation, cursed by disobedience and marred by sin manifested in so many ways: the horrible cruelty people show toward each other; mass shootings of innocent victims; the tragedy of war; the hateful and abusive words and actions of prideful, self-serving individuals; devastating natural disasters; debilitating diseases; and, ultimately, physical death for all—to name a few.

In the midst of Jeremiah's sorrow, we find the following words of hope that are the basis for one of my favorite hymns, *Great Is Thy Faithfulness*:

> "Because of the Lord's great love we are not consumed, for his compassions never fail. They are new every morning; great is your faithfulness" (Lam. 3:22–23).

Like Jeremiah, we need to recognize and appreciate God's love and faithfulness in the midst of our struggles and know that the current state of affairs won't last forever. Death is not an end-all. The good news is that the loss of perfection and curse of death placed upon the original creation are temporary. As Paul tells the Corinthians, "The last enemy to be destroyed is death" (1 Cor. 15:26). Everything will be made good once again, and our greatest enemy—death—will be defeated. Praise the Lord for that!

Here are the lyrics of a song that complements the discussion in this lesson.

"All Things Made New"

In God's time, there'll come a day
When everything's perfect in every way
All we are and all that we see
Will be created again for eternity
Why bear a burden of worry and fear
Our hope for tomorrow is clear

Chorus
We live for the promise
Of all things made new
The earth and the heavens
And all they include
We long for that place
Where the curse of the fall
Is lifted once and for all

Every moment, every day
It seems like this planet is slipping away
Life and nature out of control
As sin's consequence takes a terrible toll
But we can rely on the Word of the Lord
All will be one day restored

Bridge
No more crying, no more pain
No more death or toiling in vain
Total peace and total rest
A whole new creation that's totally blessed

***

As a wrap up, let me address a stumbling block germane to this lesson—one that causes people to reject Christianity—and that is the question: "Why does a loving and powerful God let so many bad things happen?"

First, this is not a new question; Job and the writers of Psalms asked it thousands of years ago. Second, no human has the complete answer: "Now we see things imperfectly, like puzzling reflections in a mirror, but then we will see everything with perfect clarity"(1 Cor. 13:12, NLT). Third, you can probably find hundreds of lengthy sermons online that attempt to answer this question, so I am not going to write a discourse—just give my quick and bulleted two cents worth on the subject.

- God did not create tragedy and suffering. "God saw all that he had made, and it was very good" (Gen. 1:31).
- God allowed the potential for tragedy and suffering by creating human beings with the free will to choose to love and obey or not to do so. This was his supreme plan, as opposed to creating automatons programmed to love and obey.

- We used our free will to reject God—introducing 1) the pain and suffering caused by our selfishness and arrogance and 2) the corruption of nature, resulting in the types of natural disasters that add to our pain and suffering.

- God can and does bring good from evil. "And we know that in all things God works for the good of those who love him, who have been called according to his purpose" (Rom. 8:28). I have witnessed amazing goodness, people drawn to God, and greater trust in God emerge from tragedy and pain. Look at the crucifixion of Jesus: one of the most horrific events in history, yet for the good of all humankind.

- God hates the current state of affairs and will one day get rid of all pain and suffering in a newly created heaven and earth (Isa. 65:17, 2 Pet. 3:13, Rev. 21:1).

In an interview, actor and self-proclaimed atheist Stephen Fry was asked what he would say if God really did exist and they met at the "pearly gates." Part of his response was this scathing condemnation he would direct at God: "Bone cancer in children—what's that about? How dare you! How dare you create a world in which there is such misery that is not our fault."[4] Both parts of this accusation are grossly misguided. God did not create a world of misery, and the misery that exists today is unquestionably our fault.

God hates sin, and that is why he cannot allow it in heaven. One unforgiven sin will keep us out, but Jesus took our sin upon himself so that we could stand forgiven before a righteous God. Perhaps more than anything else, however, God hates the ultimate outcome of sin for every living thing, and that is death. Praise the Lord that it also will one day be no more.

LESSON 5

Life's Goldilocks Zone Is
a Place of Contentment

It's my experience that one of faith's greatest manifestations in life is contentment. When we are certain about our eternal destiny, God's love for us, and his provision for our well-being, we can be joyfully at ease under all circumstances.

Paul Ultimately Knew What Matters

In Philippians 4:12, Paul says, "I know what it is to be in need, and I know what it is to have plenty. I have learned the secret of being content in any and every situation, whether well fed or hungry, whether living in plenty or in want."

Paul experienced the extremes of life. Although we are not given many details, his life as Saul before conversion was probably pretty good. His combined Jewish heritage and Roman citizenship most likely offered a comfortable and prestigious lifestyle. Then came the road to Damascus where he met Jesus, and everything changed.

> "Five times I received from the Jews the forty lashes minus one. Three times I was beaten with rods, once I was pelted with stones, three times I was shipwrecked, I spent a night and a day in the open sea. I have been constantly on the move. I have been in danger from rivers, in danger from bandits, in danger from my fellow Jews, in danger from Gentiles, in danger in the city, in danger in the country, in danger at sea, and in danger from false believers. I have labored and toiled and have often gone without sleep. I have known hunger and thirst and have often gone without food. I have been cold and naked" (2 Cor. 11:24–27).

What a sharp contrast to his life before Jesus. Paul knew that contentment does not result from power, riches, and status but from a deep and personal relationship with God. "What is more, I consider everything a loss because of the surpassing worth of knowing Christ Jesus my Lord, for whose sake I have lost all things. I consider them garbage that I may gain Christ" (Phil. 3:8).

My First Lesson in Contentment

As I share my story on contentment, I must say up front that I have never experienced anything close to Paul's physical and emotional trauma. I have always been blessed with sufficiency of material needs and cannot comment from the perspective of desperation. However, I do have some experience at the other end of the spectrum that has taught me a powerful life lesson.

I haven't seen one lately, but years ago I saw cars—especially expensive ones—carrying the bumper sticker: "He who dies with the most toys wins." Today, I can view this attitude as a shallow and meaningless perspective on life. Twenty years ago, I chuckled at the notion but inside was kind of living that lie. I had plenty, but I still wanted more. A part of me wanted what the top movie stars, athletes, and business executives had, and that was more than enough.

My first small conviction came in a sermon by a man whom I consider a dear friend and mentor. Rarely do I remember anything from sermons decades ago, but I will always remember his labeling of people who lacked contentment as "Lexus drivers." At the time, I drove a Lexus—not the biggest or fanciest one, but a Lexus nonetheless. On that particular day, I did not want anyone seeing me exit the church parking lot in my car. Although to this day, I remember that twinge of guilt, it didn't have a major impact on my attitude at the time. The life-changing event would come a few years later.

The Worst Year Ever

Let me tell you the story of the most miserable year of my life. At least that's what I thought until I realized that this particular year taught me a lesson about greed and contentment that would shape the rest of my life. Now, I consider it one of the most important years I've ever lived.

In the late 1990s, I was reaching the two-decade point at a company I helped grow from a start-up with about twenty people to a five-hundred-person, $50 million enterprise. I was a vice president and program manager, and I had a good salary and manageable stress level. If there was one area of discord with the company, it was that my twenty years of service had not been financially rewarded to the degree I had hoped. And this small disenchantment created an itch to perhaps explore other opportunities.

In the meantime, we were entering the period of the historic and speculative dotcom bubble, and a local Internet start-up was getting attention because of its potentially valuable patent and technology for digital media distribution. To make this long part of the story short, I was lured away from the security and stability of my job of twenty years to become chief operating officer of this start-up for a modest salary and a boatload of stock options. Finally, here was my *get-rich-quick* opportunity.

The first year was great as we built some amazing technology and started to sell our product. The stock value saw a meteoric rise, but most of my shares were restricted from sale. Then, it all happened: 9/11 attack, stock market crash, advertising revenues (our main source of income) drying up completely. Things went downhill quickly. I failed to realize the huge prosperity I had envisioned, and because of my position on the company's board of directors, angry investors threatened litigation to take away everything I and my family owned. Co-workers at my former company who, in faith, had followed me to work at this new company were now without jobs. I found myself in court, trying to defend the company's president, who was being sued by both investors and employees. I couldn't eat or sleep, my marriage was suffering, and though I could never think of taking my own life, it occurred to me more than once that the world might just be better off without me.

God, of course, intervened as he always does. I skirted lawsuits and got a new job, which turned out to be a great twilight career. But most importantly, I realized that all those verses in the Bible about contentment were absolutely true.

America's Disease

What I have been talking about is what the Bible calls coveting, pure and simple, and it is a sin forbidden by the tenth commandment. Our society is plagued by this sin today. You only have to look at the aggregate personal debt being carried by the U.S. population. These numbers are changing all the time, but as of this writing, the total credit card debt in the U.S. is about three-quarters of a trillion dollars, with an average debt of almost $16,000 for each indebted household.

I believe that many in this country know they can't be rich, but they try to live like they were rich. Credit cards have been around for well over a half a century now, and unfortunately, some see them as free money, allowing pursuit of the pleasure while delaying the pain of the payment. Americans suffer from a disease I call celebrity envy: maybe I can't be Tom Cruise or Beyonce Knowles in the entertainment world, Bill Gates or Mark Zuckerberg in the business world, Warren Buffet or George Soros in the investment world, or LeBron James or Tom Brady in the sports world, but I can sure live like them. Bankruptcy laws and debt negotiation have only stoked the "have it now, pay for it later (or never)" fire. When TV commercials tout settling a $100,000 debt or IRS obligation for pennies on the dollar, you might as well go for it.

And by the way, it's not only those who have too little that crave more. Some of the richest and most successful people in the world are the least content. There is always more to be gained; and how to spend, hoard, or protect what they have can be—and usually is—a constant source of worry and discontentment. Just look at how many celebrities possessing everything the world can offer have ended their lives by their own hand, either violently or by substance abuse.

The Bottom Line on Materialism

A while back, I read an article about a baseball player who landed the biggest contract in history. His per year, per inning, and per at-bat earnings were stunning, but the one that hit home the most was his per game salary. He would be making more in a single game than I would make in a year after forty years of working very hard and honing important business, management, and engineering skills. More in a three-hour game than me in a year! And he would be back for another game the next day.

There was a time when this math would have really bothered me, filled me with envy, and made me greedy. Today, it doesn't faze me in the least. One reason is that God has taught me a very important lesson about money, greed, and contentment.

The Bible does not say that money is the root of all evil. It is the "love of money that is the root of all kinds of evil" (1 Tim. 6:10). The love of money, which can easily be manifested as greed and envy, can practically destroy us as it nearly did me. On the other hand, money itself can do a lot of good in this world; and I can now say, with all sincerity, that I get more joy from using my financial resources for worthy causes than I do from spending it on myself. At this point in life, I am happy to report that I am content; greed and envy are things of the past.

Other Goldilocks Zones

Although my focus has been on the materialistic Goldilocks zone, there are other human attributes that have a similar zone—among them intelligence, natural talent, appearance, leadership, and athletic prowess. I would say that God has put me squarely in the median of all of them and for good reason. I can recall times in my life when, as a result of what I thought were my own efforts, I rose above my mediocrity in some of these areas; and I found pride and egotism creeping into my walk and my talk. Pride and egotism are the antitheses of the desired attribute of humility, to which all Christians should aspire. There's more on that to come in lesson 9.

One final thing: in 2 Corinthians 12, we read that God permitted a thorn in Paul's flesh to keep him from becoming conceited. Likewise, I have a "thorn in the flesh" that keeps me from becoming conceited. Paul didn't say what his was and neither will I. But suffice it to say, it has kept me from becoming arrogant, and that's a very good thing.

I think blessing counting is a byproduct of contentment (and vice versa), and the following lyrics were written at a time of particular contentment in my life.

"Blessings Counted"

Dawn breaking, life waking
God sends a brand new day
Thanksgiving for living
Should fill our hearts with praise
Still many with plenty
Desire only more
Their pleasures and treasures
Are all they waken for

Bridge
Such joy is sacrificed
When we fail to realize
God's blessings day by day
Are right before our eyes

TEN THINGS I WISH I'D KNOWN WHEN I WAS YOUNGER:
A CHRISTIAN LIFE PERSPECTIVE

Chorus
Blessings counted, one and all
Lift our spirits, break each fall
Set our hearts on things to come
Not the temporary ones
Blessings counted can somehow
Comfort through the here and now
Till we greet the glorious day
Eternal blessings light our way

Our measure of treasure
Is blessing from on high
Provisions from heaven
No wealth could ever buy

***

I conclude this lesson with a challenge to follow me in a periodic ritual. Take a few minutes during a walk or other quiet time to articulate how you have been blessed during that day, that week, that month, or across the years. There are plenty of blessings to count when you put your mind to it, and I think you will find great contentment in realizing how much you already have and how little else you really need.

LESSON 6

Scatter Plenty of Seeds and Some Are Bound to Grow

"Hi, friend, let me tell you about Jesus." How many have walked up to a perfect stranger and delivered that line? I'm guessing the majority of you have not. I have known some people who do this and are perfectly at ease with the approach. God bless them; they are probably bringing some immediate fruit to the kingdom. On the other hand, some on the receiving end may view this approach as challenging or even hostile and may be turned off completely to the Gospel message.

I admit I am not always comfortable with this type of in-your-face witnessing, especially with friends and acquaintances—although I do it sometimes with strangers. Yet it is the command of Jesus himself to go and make disciples of all nations (Matt. 28:19) and to be salt and light in the world (Matt. 5:13-14). So are there ways to fulfill this great commission that are effective while perhaps being less confrontational? I believe there are a variety of ways to share the Word and love of Jesus, and this part of the book discusses some of my lessons learned over the years in terms of ways to scatter the seeds of the Gospel message. But first, a few opening remarks.

Witnessing Is Not Optional

Years ago, I spoke in a church with an interesting sign over the door. It said, "You Are Now Entering Your Mission Field." This sign was not over the church entrance, but over the exit. It was there to remind all those leaving the church building that the mission field is not inside the building walls but is the world outside of the building.

Jesus doesn't say to be his witnesses to a lost world if you are comfortable doing it or if it fits into your schedule. It's a mandatory activity for every believer. Witnessing for Christ doesn't have to be difficult, and believe it or not, it doesn't have to bring immediate results. In fact, producing results is not our job. 1 Corinthians 3:6 says, "I [Paul] planted the seed, Apollos watered it, but God has been making it grow." It's God's job to harvest the fruit. Ours is to plant and water the seeds.

I contend that there are many types of seeds to scatter and lots of ways to scatter them. And unlike the seeds you plant in your garden—you would never plant a pumpkin seed if you want a cabbage to grow—the seeds of witnessing all mature into the same fruit: a born again person in Jesus and hopefully a life of service. I also believe that the more seeds you scatter, the more will ultimately grow.

No Soul Is the Same

Just like the planting of garden seeds, there are contributing factors in planting spiritual seeds. Three of the four Gospels (Matt. 13, Mark 4, and Luke 8) contain the parable of the sower, which illustrates that some hearts are fertile soil for the Word of God. Other hearts are not, as the parable describes, but that doesn't stop the sower from sowing seeds. Likewise, the potential for results or lack thereof shouldn't influence our seed-scattering efforts.

Also, like plant seeds, varying amounts of time, water, and sunlight are necessary for the optimal growth of Gospel seeds. I have known some people whose receptiveness was instantaneous and others who came to Christ years later. The legendary World War II hero, Jimmy Doolittle, didn't come to a saving faith in Jesus until his late eighties, although he was certainly exposed to the Gospel earlier. He then became a faithful servant of the Lord until his death at age ninety-six.

For some, the first seed planted needs to be watered liberally and frequently to make it grow. For others, it only takes light infrequent sprinkling. For some, long, intense, and uninterrupted pondering is required for growth. I liken this to a plant in the shade. For others, frequent reminders and re-exposure to the message (that is, lots of sunlight) are required for growth. Sometimes, the first seed dies, and a new seed needs to be planted, possibly several before one takes root.

The point is that every heart is different, and only God knows what it will take to ultimately harvest the fruit of a soul. Again, this is not part of our job description. We are tasked only with sowing and watering seeds, and there are many types of seeds and many methods of scattering them.

Before I move on, however, let me add an up-front caveat to the discussion of seed types. Because what follows includes some of my personal witnessing methods, one may be inclined to think I am being prideful of my own accomplishments—so-called tooting of my own horn. This couldn't be farther from the truth. I confess my efforts are pitifully small compared with the full time pastors, missionaries, and evangelists in this world. My intent is solely to share some witnessing ideas and motivate others to get engaged in the process and to, perhaps, hone my own skills in the sharing.

Seeds of the Word

This first type of seed may seem obvious, and in many cases, it stands on its own as an all-sufficient witness. "For the Word of God is alive and active. Sharper than any double-edged sword, it penetrates even to dividing soul and spirit, joints and marrow; it judges the thoughts and attitudes of the heart" (Heb. 4:12).

I have been a member of the Gideons International since 1986. The singular mission of this organization of Christian men and women is to win people to the Lord through the distribution of scriptures. Since the organization was founded in 1899, over two billion copies of God's Word have been handed out around the world free of charge to the recipients, and the number of distributed scriptures continues to increase every year.

I have participated in many organized distributions, spoken in churches to raise funding, and given out Bibles and New Testaments at places like prisons, schools, and on the streets of the city in which I live. If being part of such a selfless organization is appealing to you, I suggest visiting www.gideons.org for more information.

However, being a member of an organization certainly isn't required to sow the seeds of the Word. Bibles, New Testaments, and Christian tracts are available from many sources, including Amazon, and the smaller items can be carried around in the pocket, purse, or car's glove compartment. For those who appear to be materially hurting, I combine the handing out of a scripture or tract with a little money to meet the physical need as well. Sometimes, this act leads to a conversation during which additional sharing is possible. But it's not necessary; the Word of God stands on its own.

I go on frequent short-term mission trips and will talk about this more in lesson 7 on comfort zones. In terms of sowing seeds of the Word, I almost always visit Spanish-speaking countries on these trips: Mexico, Honduras, Costa Rica, and Ecuador. And I always carry plenty of Spanish New Testaments to give out. Some of the biggest smiles I have ever seen are on the faces of people into whose hands has just been placed a copy of the Word of God in their own language.

There are many other witnessing tools, such as John 3:16 coins, which can be left almost anywhere: for the server in a restaurant (alongside the monetary tip), for housekeepers on the last day of a hotel stay, for store clerks, and the list goes on.

Of course, having these witnessing tools at your disposal (for example, on your person or in your car) is key to using them. If they're not available, they can't be given out. If they are available and you are aware that they are, I believe you will be more inclined to use them.

Seeds of Personal Experience

All Christians have unique stories about how they came to salvation and how faith changed their lives. Perhaps the story includes a God-inspired journey from desperation to recovery. Maybe a physical life was saved by a miracle. Maybe an unanticipated answer to prayer brought joy and peace in the midst of chaos that would have destroyed faithless lives.

Personal stories are a great witness. "Let me tell you what God did for me" is a great way to start a conversation and possibly open a heart. Preparation isn't necessarily required, but it may help to have some structure to your story, including things like the following:

- What your life was like before becoming a Christian
- How the things you previously thought were important let you down
- How and when you were exposed to Christianity
- What motivated you to believe
- Specifics about how your life changed after accepting Christ

Short and sweet is recommended. Practice in telling your story is recommended. The book of Acts includes the testimony of Paul, which is a great example of a life totally changed by Christ, and it is a great story to emulate. Your goals should be for the listener to have a clear understanding of how and why you became a Christian, to understand how Christ in your life has made a difference, and to know that the same results are available to him or her.

Here's the catch with seed sowing by personal experience alone. For those floundering with no direction or conviction, your story may be all that's required to prompt a response to the calling of the one true God.

However, there are many in this world who will claim similar enlightenment and positive life change through experiencing the nirvana of Buddhism or connecting with Allah during Islamic evening prayers or as Scientology holds, realizing salvation by attaining brotherhood with the universe.

Here is where biblical knowledge and good apologetics are necessary to complement your story. How do you know Jesus was raised from the dead? How can you be sure the Gospels are reliable? What makes you think the Bible is more trustworthy than the Koran or Book of Mormon? Why is Christianity the best explanation for what's happening in the world? Your story may be compelling, but the reinforcement of your story with God's truth is the indisputable force that will overcome intellectual barriers to Christianity.

Seeds of Doubt in a Belief System

This type of seed sowing is a natural extension of the previous discussion. An acquaintance of mine in a church I attended twenty years ago said that his favorite witnessing question was this: "What if you're wrong about your beliefs?" Of course, this is not how the conversation starts out. First, you need to get around to a spiritual discussion. Everyone believes in something, and some are willing to share their beliefs. It's amazing how many alternatives to Bible-based Christianity you will hear.

Many believe in multiple ways to get to heaven. Their contention is that Bible-believing Christians are narrow-minded and even prejudicial in suggesting that accepting Christ's work on the cross is the only path to forgiveness of sin and salvation. Of course, these are not our words but God's.

Some contend that only a terrible and intolerant God would exclude those who have never heard about Jesus, and some believe in God but want no part of him because they think he is disconnected from the pain and suffering in the world.

The list of belief systems goes on and on, but assuming the discussion with a nonbeliever gets to this point, the simple question follows: "What if you're wrong?" If the immediate response isn't "Well I'm not wrong," the significance of an answer can be explained. And it's kind of win-win for the believer.

If I as a believer am wrong—oh well—with our last breaths, we both pass into nothingness with our remains becoming worm feed. At least I will have lived a life of immense joy and hope in an amazing (albeit imaginary) eternity. However if you are wrong, when I pass from this life, I will stand justified before a holy God who, by his promise, will admit me to heaven. You, on the other hand, won't be going to heaven. Yes, you will stand before the throne of judgment. And despite your appeals—I was a good person, I believed in you, I went to church all the time, I prayed every day, what about those billions who never heard of Jesus?—the God who gave his all for you by sacrificing his own Son will dismiss you with "I never knew you, depart from me" (Matt. 7:23, KJV).

Doubt in a belief system can prompt some to at least consider the claims of Christ, especially when they realize the magnitude of accountability for being wrong.

Seeds of Compassion

I enjoy going to Las Vegas a couple times a year. I don't gamble, but I do enjoy the sights, shows, and Red Rock Canyon hikes. Lately, something else I have enjoyed doing is stapling $5 bills to Billy Graham's *Steps to Peace with God* tracts and taking them down to the Strip. There are many pedestrian bridges going over the busy streets, and they are a haven for the less fortunate. There is always much appreciation for this small bit of attention to both physical and spiritual needs. And an opportunity to share further with a New Testament or discussion of God's plan of salvation often follows this small act of kindness.

Some have suggested that I be selective about this giving, to try to discern whether the money might be spent on alcohol or drugs. I say that's not my concern. That user, abuser, or addict may have the greatest need for spiritual healing. Who knows, the next "high" might drive that person to open the tract or Testament and see the light for the first time. And by the way, God already knows whether they will or not.

Christian-based child sponsorship organizations are marvelous ways to show compassion, one child at a time. There are several of these organizations that have high standards of accountability, but I happen to sponsor children through an organization that, appropriate to this subsection, is called Compassion International. I have been blessed to sponsor many children over the years and have even met a couple of them.

Child sponsorship reminds me of Loren Eiseley's starfish story, which most readers have probably heard but is worth repeating in a slightly edited version here:

> "While wandering a deserted beach, a man saw a boy in the distance picking up and throwing things. As the man approached, he saw that the boy was throwing starfish abandoned on the sand by the tide back into the sea. When he was close enough, he asked him why he was working so hard at this task, because there were thousands of starfish on the beach, and he couldn't possibly make a difference. The boy smiled as he picked up the next starfish. Hurling it back into the sea he said, 'It makes a difference for this one.'"[5]

Child sponsorship through a reputable Christ-centered organization is a lot like throwing starfish into the sea: it is impacting lives one at a time.

No matter what method we use to show compassion, we are influencing God's kingdom one life at a time. But as the following lyrics suggest, I believe it's the power in the name of God that is both the motivator of the giver's action and the instrument of the receiver's response.

"The Power of His Name"

This world is filled with pain and sorrow
With loneliness and deep despair
So many people face tomorrow
Without a hope, without a prayer
But there's a message
Those of faith must carry

Chorus
There is a light in Jesus
The strength to carry on
A ray of hope to cling to
When every shred of hope is gone
And as his messengers
We carry forth his flame
One at a time, we'll see lives changed
By the power of his name

Our words must show the Lord's compassion
So others know he lives in us
But more than words our faith in action
Will demonstrate the Savior's love
And through our words and deeds
The world will know him

Bridge
His name a sanctuary
His name a peace
His name from chains of bondage
A sure release

His name a joy in living
That fills the soul
The only name that makes us whole

Seeds of Righteous Defense

For several years after I accepted Christ, I retained a bit of a foul mouth. Taking the Lord's name in vain was commonplace on board nuclear submarines, and regrettably, I fell in line. One day, while visiting a friend's family, his mother made this comment: "I love the way you say g**d***." Notice that I won't even spell the word out anymore, let alone say it. At that instant in time, I was mortified to learn that one of my apparent distinctive attributes was the creativeness and eloquence I put into swearing. I'm not sure how long after this incident I made a commitment to never take the Lord's name in vain again, but I can say, with certainty, that I have not done it for at least the past thirty years and never will again.

The names of members of the Trinity—God, Jesus, and the Holy Spirit—are truly holy, and defending those names can be a witnessing tool, if done gently and with kindheartedness.

A female coworker had all brothers growing up and worked in a predominantly male environment all her adult life. Fitting in often meant becoming "one of the guys," and becoming one of the guys meant talking tough and dirty like they did. When I first started working with her, the name of God was never spoken without an accompanying "damn," and she used this combination of words as a noun, adjective, interjection, and just about every other English part of speech.

One day, it was just the two of us when she used the words, and I finally said something. I told her that I would never say this in a larger gathering, but between her and me, I was a Christian. And frankly, taking the name of Lord in vain was offensive to me and certainly to him. Her immediate response was a nod and an okay, but over the subsequent weeks and months, her speech pattern changed, not just when she was with me but in group settings as well. Early on, she would start into the phrase, then catch herself and substitute a "gosh darnit" or a "dad gummit." Over time, her use of the phrase disappeared completely. We parted ways a while ago, and I don't know if she is a Christian or not. But there is no doubt that defending the holy name of God had an impact and was, therefore, a unique type of witness.

Service people often come into my house for various routine maintenance items. One day, during an election season, I had the news on TV, and one of the guys went into a rant about one of the candidates. G**d*** *last name* this and g**d*** *last name* that, and it went on and on. I interrupted and pointed to an item I have hanging on the wall near my front door—a beautiful wooden cross from Honduras with the name Jesus carved in the beams. I said that the person whose name was on my wall ruled this house, and he didn't like his Father's name used like that and neither did I.

For the next several minutes, as the service was being completed, the apologies were manifold. During a subsequent service a couple months later, it was obvious the conversation was still in memory. The door was opened to give the man a copy of the New Testament. Hopefully, God is speaking to him.

I know part of my personal sanctification process has been the realization that God's name is holy and not to be used inappropriately. Now, whenever someone takes the Lord's name in vain in my presence, I am offended. Even when people offhandedly or jokingly throw around the phrase—and I only state it here for the sake of my point—"Oh my God," it disturbs me as well. I have a friend who once said that every time people use this expression, it's like placing a crank call to the Lord because they have no intention of speaking to him and should he answer the call, they certainly have no intention of listening to what he has to say.

As you might imagine, I have written a song about this subject.

"Holy Is the Name"

There is one name above all others
Holy is the name
A name of hope for all the ages
Holy is the name

Chorus
And I'll get down on my knees to lift it up
Stand in awe of its infinite worth
And I'll proclaim the name of Jesus until
It's known through all the earth

There is one name that rescues sinners
Holy is the name
That changes death to life eternal
Holy is the name

Bridge
All joy, all peace, all strength, all love
Are found in that wonderful name
And all who call upon it
Will be forever changed

You are my God and my Creator
Holy is your name
You are my Lord and my Redeemer
Holy is your name

Last Chorus
And I'll get down on my knees to lift you up
Stand in awe of your infinite worth
And I'll proclaim your name, O Jesus, until
It's known through all the earth

Seeds of Inspiration

Matthew 24:14 says, "And this Gospel of the kingdom will be preached in the whole world as a testimony to all nations." A hundred years ago, one would be hard pressed to imagine how this could possibly happen, no matter how many missionaries took to the field. Today, with worldwide TV and radio broadcasts and ubiquitous Internet streaming of video and audio, that prediction of two thousand years ago doesn't seem so far-fetched.

I have personally been the beneficiary of these and other twenty-first-century technologies. As I mentioned in the preface, I know basic guitar and piano through self-teaching—read that as no musical training. Well, that's not 100 percent true. My mother sent me to a piano lesson once, and I walked out ten minutes after it started and promised to run away from home if she ever sent me back to that teacher. She didn't, and that was the end of my formal training.

But getting back to the technology point, musical composition tools of the digital age such as sequencing, virtual sounds, and musical loops have provided the means to get the songs inside my head (which I truly believe are inspired) into production, despite my mediocre musical chops.

Furthermore, the emergence of personalized Internet radio services—mine happens to be Jango radio—has allowed independent artists like myself to get airplay around the world interspersed among well-known and established artists.

I've had close to 100,000 airplays worldwide, many in countries you wouldn't think are receptive to Christian music. I have a growing fan base of thousands and have received countless comments of support from these fans. No one can know what God is doing through obedience in planting these seeds of inspiration. I pray in heaven I meet someone who comes up and says your song pointed me to Jesus or caused me to give up self-destructive ways or encouraged me to devote more energy to kingdom work. Who knows what my meager airplay has done? God surely does.

Seeds of Lifestyle

I don't think lifestyle evangelism can stand on its own as a Christian witness because even nonbelievers are capable of wholesome words and acts of kindness. However, in conjunction with some of the other seeds, it can be a powerful testimony to God at work in us.

In contrast, someone who claims to be a Christian and doesn't act the part through lifestyle can turn people off to the Gospel. Can anyone say he or she has never seen an outraged and reckless driver in a car with one of those fish symbols on the back?

A favorite verse of mine is Matthew 5:16: "...Let your light shine before others, that they may see your good deeds and glorify your Father in heaven." As the following song suggests, all of us are to *shine on* on a daily basis.

"Shine On"

> There is a constant conflict
> Between the wide and narrow way
> A struggle for the hearts and minds
> Of people every day
> And though it seems most of the time
> The wrong wins over right
> Our calling as believers
> Is to be beacons in the night
>
> Chorus
> Shine on, shine on
> Let our light shine before men
> So that all will praise the Father
> And know that we belong to him
> Shine on, shine on
> Through every word and deed
> Our light is what this world in darkness
> Desperately needs

As we navigate life's journey
Are we lost within the crowd?
Living silent walks with Jesus
Or are we living faith out loud?
With a witness shining strong and bright
Not from any light within
But from a bold reflection
Of the brilliant light in him

Bridge
You may think one light alone
Has very little worth
But millions shining all at once
Will illuminate the earth

***

When we say yes to God, we're not supposed to sit on the sidelines and be bystanders. Christianity is not a spectator sport. We are compelled by Matthew 28:19 to "go and make disciples of all nations" and by Matthew 5:13–14 to be "the salt of the earth" and "the light of the world." Remember that our job is just planting and watering seeds, and God will do the rest. We may never know the fruit resulting from our seed planting until we get to heaven. Here are a couple more songs that illustrate these important points.

"Salt and Light"

There's a battle taking shape today
Between what's right and what's wrong
And everybody needs to make a choice
Which side we want to be on
We're either for God or
We're against God
We either love or hate his Word
The lines between are never blurred
We hold his truth up high
Or we stand idly by
Well I have made my choice
Time to make some righteous noise

Chorus
I will be salt and light
A beacon in the night
A messenger of right
A loyal soldier in the fight
I will be salt and light
Turn blindness into sight
Defend God's truth with all my might

Though it's not easy being on God's side
It's what we're called to do
Despite the obstacles we find along
The path that's narrow and true
There always comes a time
When we must all decide
Where we will fall in line

And where our true allegiance lies
When conflict comes
Many will turn and run
But when all others fall away
On God's side I'll always stay

Bridge
Salt and light (repeated)
Seasoning each word with grace
Illuminating darkened space
Sharing precious words of life
Every morning, noon and night

"In Glory's Perfect Light"

The pebbles of our witness hit the water
The ripples of our work spread far and wide
And though we get a glimpse
Of the kingdom role we play
We never see the total difference
That we make, but...

Chorus
In glory's perfect light
It all will be made clear
The bounds of mortal knowledge
Forever disappear
The fruit of every life
Will finally be revealed
How big, how deep, how wide
Has been our mission field

There's faith and trust in every seed we scatter
'Cause where they finally land we may not know
Others give them water
And God will make them grow
In this life, we rarely reap
All that we sow, but…

Bridge
Heaven knows how many lives
We'll touch along the way
But we'll discover all God's done
Through us one blessed day

LESSON 7

Our Comfort Zones Are Not That Comfortable

I went on my first mission trip at the age of fifty-six, the same age at which my father passed into eternity—definitely too late but early enough to be able to participate in many more. The type of mission trip I'm talking about is not the kind where you spread the Word of God at rallies or hand out Bibles, though that work is important. I am talking about work trips, where you help out a person, family, or group by building a house, painting a school, or laying a church foundation.

To Give or To Go

I was always content to give money to missions, figuring that was sufficient to reach the world for Christ, but I was wrong. That was just an excuse to stay inside my comfort zone. When I finally broke out of that zone and went on my first mission trip, which was to Honduras, I discovered two things. First, mission work is addictive, and once you get the bug, you'll want to keep doing it. In my opinion, it's one of the most rewarding things a Christian can do. Second, when you are blessing the less fortunate in material and spiritual ways, you are receiving an equal or even greater blessing.

I don't relish doing chores around the house because that work is for me. But put me in the mission field working for a needy family or a third world church or a school for underprivileged kids, and I become a work machine because I am working for the recipient of the effort and for God.

The Fruit of Going

I could devote many pages to my mission field experiences, but let me share the story of just one trip to illustrate my point.

Homes of Hope (HoH) is a segment of the international ministry, Youth With A Mission, commonly called YWAM. HoH partners with churches, businesses, universities, and other organizations to build homes for needy families in Mexico, the Dominican Republic, and Costa Rica, as well as other places, but primarily in the northern Baja area of Mexico. The partnering organization raises funds for construction. Then, a team of fifteen to twenty-five travels to the local YWAM campus and, together with staff members, builds a modest home in two days. So much can be said about this amazing organization, and if you want to know more, please visit their website:

http://www.ywamsandiegobaja.org/
homesofhope

I had gone on three HoH builds with First Rate, a Texas investment solutions firm that energetically lives out its core values of love, give, serve, and enjoy. After these trips, I would show pictures and give reports in my church, but I wanted to do more. So I talked with my pastor about our church doing its own build, and he said, "That's a great idea. You're in charge." During the nine months of organizing and preparing, I frequently made the point to participants that they would be blessed and that they would come back home as changed people.

We headed to Mexico on October 23, 2015 and worked very hard for two days to complete a sturdy, stick-built home that would impact a family for generations. At the emotional house dedication, as the keys were being passed around the circle of builders and words were spoken to the family, tissues were insufficient. Buckets would have been more appropriate for the tears that flowed. The Cuenco-Barrobon family was overwhelmed. After living for so long on a dirt floor with some plywood cobbled together for protection from the elements, they now had a beautiful home with beds, tables and chairs, electricity, and a stove. Both former and new homes can be seen in this picture.

As the team lead, I was privileged to have the last words and pass the keys to the family. Among my words to the family were these: "The Bible says that we are to love others because God loved us first. Everyone here loves you, and this home is an expression of that love because we are loved so much by Jesus, who died to give us eternal life. And that is why his name is displayed prominently in your new home." I was referring to a small wooden cross with the name of Jesus carved into the beams, very similar to the one I have in my own home. I hung it on their new wall as the final punctuation to two days of work for God and this family.

After the dedication, our build team had to head back to the HoH campus, but our YWAM host stayed with the family a bit longer. This family had sometimes prayed to God, but with no substantive answers to their physical needs, there were doubts about his personal love for them. Therefore, they had a bit of agnosticism. Our host reported that on this day, when their prayers were answered through a group of sixteen strangers from the United States who gave up a weekend to show up at their property and build them a house, the entire family accepted Christ as their Lord and Savior.

That evening, my team had a circle of sharing about what the experience meant to each of them. Many in the group commented that although I had repeatedly told them they would be incredibly blessed and changed, they couldn't really imagine what that would feel like until they had been through the experience.

***

Wrapping up, I should say that you don't have to go to a third world country to get involved in mission work. There is plenty of need and there are plenty of outreach opportunities here in the U.S. Work at a soup kitchen or shelter, be a companion to the elderly, do foster care, etc., etc., etc. Just leave that comfort zone behind for a while every now and then. When you do, you will realize it's not that comfortable.

Most of us in this country are incredibly blessed. It's easy to take what we have for granted, and we can get rattled when our perfect little worlds get the least bit out of alignment. My advice to all readers is to periodically do something for the 95+ percent of the world that doesn't have it so good. You will be so much more appreciative of what you have, and you will be blessed beyond belief. That blessing is impossible to comprehend until you have taken the first step.

And to add to the witnessing discussion of the previous lesson, a recent mission trip is a great conversation starter. People love talking about travel, and mission trips certainly fall into that category. Most will be very interested in your adventure. Asked or not, you can get around to why you do it, something like: "God has blessed me so much, I want to pay it forward and bless others."

"Oh, what has he done for you?" you are asked. And the conversation begins…

I close this lesson with two song lyrics, each with a different take on getting beyond the boundaries of our comfort zones and finding some kingdom work to do.

"Out of My World"

There is a place I know
That I can call my own
It's always safe and warm
My private comfort zone
It's sheltered from the burden
I'm called to bear
Well I think it's time
I got away from there

TEN THINGS I WISH I'D KNOWN WHEN I WAS YOUNGER:
A CHRISTIAN LIFE PERSPECTIVE

Chorus
Help me get out of my world and into yours
Help me to seek out and find your open doors
To live for the blessing
That comes from possessing
A heart that won't hide anymore
Help me get out of my world and into yours

Your world is not like mine
There's tragedy and pain
A billion searching souls
Who've never heard your name
The fields are ready
But the workers are few
Now it's finally time to do
What I must do

Bridge
Out of my world and into yours
Lord I pray for a way to your world every day

"Life Can Be More Than That"

Rise and shine, another day
Jump into the rat race once again
Make your money, pay the bills
Get a couple thrills in now and then
Now something's tugging at your heart
Calling for a brand new start
But when the day is over nothing's changed

Chorus
Don't you know it's true
Life can be more than that
Maybe time for you
To finally throw your hat
Into the ring and get engaged
Find your purpose, turn the page
Write a brand new chapter
In the story of your life

The emptiness is hard to feed
Your things don't satisfy the need within
Where you live and what you drive
Will never make you feel alive so then
You think of living out your faith
But something's always in the way
So back inside your comfort zone you head

Bridge
You stumble through the weeks and years
Just searching for a way
To try to climb out of the rut you're in
But good intentions fade away
And round and round the maze you go again

LESSON 8

God Really Is In Charge

The 1988 hit, "Don't Worry, Be Happy," by Bobby McFerrin was a fun little number with a message that encourages everyone to not be overly concerned when bad things are happening in life. This is good advice from a medical standpoint, as excessive stress has been shown to seriously impact health and even cause premature death. But there is also a biblical basis for this advice.

As part of his sermon on the mount, Jesus shared these words on worry:

> "Therefore I tell you, do not worry about your life... Can any of you by worrying add a single hour to your life?... But seek first his kingdom and his righteousness, and all these things will be given to you as well. Therefore do not worry about tomorrow, for tomorrow will worry about itself.

Each day has enough trouble of its
own" (Matt. 6:25, 27, 33–34).

So we're not supposed to worry? That's surely easier said than done! Accepting God's gift of salvation—there's nothing to it. It's a free gift for those willing to receive it. Getting involved in church and allowing the Holy Spirit to lead us toward obedience and good works are a bit harder but doable. However, following the above advice on worry is one of the hardest things I have ever tried to do. I could never accomplish it in my own strength, and I struggle with it even today.

I am and continue to be a Type A personality: ambitious, goal oriented, competitive, impatient, everything planned to the nanosecond, meticulous, energetic, and urgent in all that I do. In fact, if there were such a thing as a Type A+ personality, I would be it.

That said, I'm reluctantly learning the lesson that God is in charge of everything, and learning this lesson has been difficult but liberating. Why? Because I know that no matter what happens in my life, I win. I've been redeemed by Christ, so I win. If I suffer health issues or injury, I win. If my financial means disappear, I win. If my least favorite candidate is elected to office, I (with some dismay) win. If I lose all my friends, I win. If I die (more like when I die), I win. I'm not saying any of this is fun, but in the context of eternity, these micro-issues become meaningless. God is in charge, and his thoughts and ways are infinitely beyond ours.

God Has a Plan for Every Person

Before I perform one of my songs, "Master Plan," in a concert or for special music, I ask the audience this question: "How many really enjoy life when things are going smoothly, you have your health and plenty of friends, your finances are in order, and stress is relatively low?" All the hands go up into the air. Then, I ask the follow-up question: "How many really enjoy life when you're sick as a dog or suffering from a serious injury, you're terribly lonely, you've recently lost a love one, you're barely getting by financially, or you're going through a difficult emotional or spiritual trial?" As you might guess, hardly any hands go up.

Proverbs 16:9 says, "In their hearts humans plan their course, but the Lord establishes their steps." I am convinced that whether times are good or tough, God not only knows what all of us are going through, he puts us into those situations for reasons that, oftentimes, only he understands. Maybe it's to learn an important life lesson. Maybe it's to correct a sinful behavior. Maybe we've strayed, and he is trying to draw us closer again.

I can only guess at his divine purposes, but I can testify that some of my personal journeys through valleys so low I thought I could never get out were followed by some of life's highest mountaintop experiences. The point is we should rejoice through all life's circumstances because God is working out his purposes for us in the here and now; and of course, in the end, we win!

And here's one final thought. Maybe you haven't accepted God's gift of salvation yet, but if at any point in this lifetime you will, God knows it right now. In fact, he chose you before time began to become part of his family. How's that for a plan for your life?

"Master Plan"

We grasp the good times as hard as we can
And pray the bad times go away
But trouble finds us again and again
And now and then it's here to stay
Now what the Father would like us to know
It's everything we go through that helps us to grow

Chorus
There's a time to be born, a time to die
And in between, times to laugh and to cry
A time to hurt, a time to heal
It's all a part of what makes this life real
And as we embrace the ups and the downs
A new song of praise we will sing
Thank you Lord for your master plan
'Cause in it, there's a time for everything

There'll come a day, not too long from now
When trials and tribulations cease
The sorrow ends, and God won't allow
Anything to steal our joy and peace
But for the moment, by his own design
Sunshine and storms both get their equal time

God Has a Plan for Our Country...

I am writing this section during a heated election season, when passions run deep and fervor runs high. Now, before I say what the Bible says about those in leadership positions, let me first say that I believe in capitalism, free enterprise, and small government; and I believe that these principles of governing and economics are supported by the Bible. For an in-depth look into this subject and the basis for my beliefs, I highly recommend Chad Hovind's book called *Godonomics*.

With that said, let's look at Romans 13:1: "Let everyone be subject to the governing authorities, for there is no authority except that which God has established. The authorities that exist have been established by God." What this tells me is that no matter who gets elected and how distasteful that person is in terms of my personal preference, he or she has been put there at a point in history by God to help implement his eternal plans.

I know a lot of people who have threatened to move out of the country or jump off a bridge if a certain person gets elected. I have learned that I should simply perform my civic duty to cast my vote according to my beliefs, pray God's will be done, and let him take it from there. The result is a stress level that is a lot lower than when I dreaded one not of my choosing getting elected.

...But Where Does His Plan Leave the USA?

Recognizing God is in control of governing authorities, I am still concerned about the direction of the

United States, and I fear God's plan for our country will not be to our liking. Our country was founded on biblical principles, and we have veered off path. As one example, let's briefly look at what we call "separation of church and state."

Contrary to much popular belief, this precise phrase is nowhere in the Constitution. The First Amendment statement, "Congress shall make no law respecting an establishment of religion, or prohibiting the free exercise thereof," has evolved into something entirely new over the last generation. Rather than guaranteeing the freedom *of* religion, reinterpretations of this statement now ensure the freedom *from* religion.

Prayer in schools has been deemed unconstitutional; even pausing for a moment of silence to start the school day is prohibited. Nativity scenes and crosses are banned from public property. Religious symbols have been removed from city seals. The Ten Commandments are no longer displayed in courtrooms.

I believe we need to re-examine the precarious path we have been heading down, one in which human wisdom trumps the Word of God when it comes to our words and our actions. It's a common belief that the values of our ancestors don't apply today and that ethics and behaviors are generational. But that belief couldn't be more wrong. There are moral absolutes clearly stated in the Bible; and history has proven, time and time again, that when a country strays from those absolutes, decline is imminent. As individuals, we are in need of a change of heart. Hopefully, as the number of individual hearts that return to God's truth grows, the heart of the nation will follow.

I believe we are in dire need of a revival, not just a revival of belief, but also one of obedience. God's Word speaks to all aspects of our human journey—from personal choices to family life, to engagement with others, to our eternal destinations. We need to get back into the Word of God, recognizing its divine source and following its guidance rather than the behavioral trends of current society.

It has always been a curiosity when reading scripture related to the end times that the U.S. seems to be absent from the discussion. Could it be that we are really not in the big picture when Jesus returns? I pray this is not the case.

My statement of this conviction is in the following lyrics. We all need to pray that the one true God who has blessed us so bountifully since the founding of our country does not abandon us because of our refusal to take his Word as timeless and trustworthy.

"A Nation Under God"

"In God We Trust"
Words that we can believe
A tried-and-true conviction
That's guided this great land
But it seems we've strayed
From the forefathers' dream
And chosen shaky ground
To make a stand

TEN THINGS I WISH I'D KNOWN WHEN I WAS YOUNGER:
A CHRISTIAN LIFE PERSPECTIVE

It may be time to wonder
"Are there limits to God's grace?"
When we let him in our churches
But not in any other place

Chorus
We need to live the trust our fathers lived
And walk the path that those of faith have trod
Pledge allegiance to our flag
And say those words with pride
But not forget the most important part
We're a nation under God

The choice we've made
Is to go our own way
Follow human wisdom
Instead of timeless truth
We know God's Word
But refuse to obey
Choosing to ignore
His moral absolutes
And then we ask what kind of God
Lets tragedy abound
What are we expecting
When we've kicked him out of town

Bridge
If we want to have God's blessing
Then it's time this country heard
We'll only be in his safe keeping
When we're grounded in his Word

God Has a Plan for the World

It has been said that in the big scheme of things, world history is, in reality, *His Story*, that everything revolves around Jesus Christ. After all, he is the Alpha and Omega. It is all about Jesus, and we'll discuss this more in the next lesson. So where does *His Story* take us from this point in history?

Years ago, I had a colleague who, at the time, was more mature in his Christian walk than I was. He had a very laid-back attitude toward all material things. He viewed the possessions the world coveted as meaningless and temporary. On countless occasions, when we would encounter examples of indulgence such as a beautiful mansion on the ocean or a high-end car like a Ferrari or Maserati, he would shrug and say, "Hey, it's all gonna burn."

At the time, I would smile and concur, but I didn't realize until much later the literal accuracy and significance of this casual comment. So here's the good news, the bad news, and the very good news.

The Good News and Bad News

Genesis chapters 6 through 9 discuss the worldwide flood during the time of Noah, which I believe explains much of the geology of the earth as we see it today (see lesson 10). After the flood waters receded, God made a promise to Noah, his descendants, and every living creature.

> "And God said, 'This is the sign of the covenant I am making between me and you and every living creature with you, a covenant for all generations to come: I have set my rainbow in the clouds, and it will be the sign of the covenant between me and the earth. Whenever I bring clouds over the earth and the rainbow appears in the clouds, I will remember my covenant between me and you and all living creatures of every kind. Never again will the waters become a flood to destroy all life.'"(Gen. 9:11–15).

The good news is God will never again destroy all life by water. The bad news is that there is destruction in our planet's future, the next time by fire.

> "By the same Word the present heavens and earth are reserved for fire, being kept for the day of judgment and destruction of the ungodly. The heavens will disappear with a roar; the elements will be destroyed by fire, and the earth and everything done in it will be laid bare" (2 Pet. 3:7,10).

The Very Good News

Some of the very good news falls between the above two verses in verse 9, where Peter says, "He [God] is patient with you, not wanting anyone to perish, but everyone to come to repentance." But the best news of all is that not a one of us believers will be around to experience this destruction by fire.

I love the book of Revelation. Many think it is allegorical or too difficult to understand. But I believe it presents, among other topics, a concise picture of end-time events and, with the return of Jesus, removal of the curse of Genesis 3 and the restoration of paradise—one even better than creation before its corruption by sin.

Chapters 2 and 3 of this book are seven letters to seven churches, which convey spiritual messages to individual churches of that day but also to the Church as a whole. I find it fascinating that after these two chapters, in which the churches are the focal point, the word *church* doesn't appear in chapters 4 through 18. While all God's righteous judgment is taking place, the Church—God's people in this dispensation—is nowhere to be found. "Since you have kept my command to endure patiently, I will also keep you from the hour of trial that is going to come on the whole world to test the inhabitants of the earth" (Rev. 3:10). Hallelujah to that! Wouldn't it be glorious if the rapture of the Church takes place while we are still alive?

***

To wrap up this lesson, God's eternal plan for the redemption of humankind and the restoration of all that was lost in Genesis 3 has been proceeding ceaselessly since that fateful day in the Garden of Eden. He works out his plan through people and in spite of people.

He has a remarkable plan for each person placing his or her trust in him. He has a plan for the United States, and he has a plan for the world. The plan for this dispensation will culminate in an end-time period of tribulation like the world has never seen. However, both the dead and living in Christ at the beginning of this period will be raptured to be with him. A Christ-ruled one thousand years of peace on a millennial earth will follow the Great Tribulation, and when that is over, eternity begins with "a new heaven and a new earth" (Rev. 21:1).

For the believer, eternity will be sin-free, glorious, and never boring. I enjoyed the book-turned-movie, *Heaven is for Real,* written by Todd Burpo about his son Colton's amazing journey to heaven during a near-death experience (NDE). But I have enjoyed *Imagine Heaven: Near-Death Experiences, God's Promises, and the Exhilarating Future That Awaits You* by John Burke even more because like me, Mr. Burke is an engineer. He has performed a critical analysis of hundreds of NDEs and has found amazing consistencies between experiences. In the process, he has answered some big questions about heaven and a few about hell as well. What a magnificent place heaven will be in contrast with the alternative.

As many have said and as implied in both of the below songs, the real home of the believer is not this

earth. We are merely sojourners here, awaiting and preparing for our transit to a place our still-earth-bound
minds cannot begin to comprehend.

"What We Are Made For"

Here today, gone tomorrow
Life like the weather comes and goes
Years are few, days are numbered
How many left God only knows
But if there's only the here and now
What would the purpose in living be?

Chorus
Not for today, not for tomorrow
Not for this world alone
Not for the pain, not for the sorrow
Not for a destiny unknown
What we are made for is forever
What we are made for is an eternal home

We are here for a moment
Tomorrow gives no guarantee
Maybe soon, maybe later
We'll all be bound for eternity
And when we get to the other side
There's so much waiting for you and me

TEN THINGS I WISH I'D KNOWN WHEN I WAS YOUNGER:
A CHRISTIAN LIFE PERSPECTIVE

Bridge
Not for a fleeting walk on earth
Not for a nothingness beyond
But knowing with our final breath
Our lives go on and on and on

"It's Not Home"

The earth has always been a part of me
A place of growth and opportunity
A place to raise a family
To live with faith and dignity
But there's one thing that it can never be

Chorus
It's not home
Never has been, never will be
It's not home
Though it's all I've ever known
I was made for somewhere else
A place I've yet to see
For now, the world is where I'm meant to be
But it's not home

Now my eyes are set on heaven's shore
And though I don't know all it has in store
It's the place I want to be
With Jesus for eternity
And when I'm there the world will be a memory

Bridge
Home is where the heart is
And my heart is in a place
The Lord's preparing just for me
Earth may move me, thrill me
Awe, inspire, fulfill me
But it never ever will be... home

LESSON 9

It's Not About Me;
It's All About God

I grew up as part of the "me generation." Phrases like "if it feels good do it" and "look out for number one" were part of my formative years. Popular songs echoing this philosophy included Sammy Davis Jr.'s "I've Gotta Be Me" and Whitney Houston's "One Moment in Time." This attitude seemed to be the cultural norm, and my early life fell in line with this way of thinking, which is the total antithesis of a life aligned with God's will.

In my little self-centered existence, it didn't really occur to me that I was a miniscule speck on the face of the earth, which was a miniscule speck in a massive universe, and that unless I achieved some fame or notoriety, I wouldn't even be remembered by my descendants a few generations in the future. A cancer diagnosis in 2007 woke me up to the fact that my earthly existence could be terminated at any point in time.

I wish I'd figured out at a younger age that it's not about me; it's all about God and, by extension, others.

Of Ants, Humans, and God

I think many people, including some believers, do not appreciate the awesomeness of God's knowledge and power. Some tend to visualize him as a finite entity and put bounds on his capabilities. Some perceive him as old and out-of-tune with the complexities of modern life. Some don't believe he can comprehend current technology. Here are some verses that help us understand our amazing God:

> "For my thoughts are not your thoughts, neither are your ways my ways, declares the Lord. As the heavens are higher than the earth, so are my ways higher than your ways, and my thoughts than your thoughts" (Isa. 55:8–9).

> "Do you not know? Have you not heard? The Lord is the everlasting God, the Creator of the ends of the earth. He will not grow tired or weary, and his understanding no one can fathom" (Isa. 40:28).

> "Great is our Lord, and mighty in power; his understanding has no limit" (Ps. 147:5).

To begin to understand the enormous gap between us and God, visualize a colony of ants, busily doing their work and totally unaware of the superior intellect and awareness attached to the descending foot about to crush them out of existence. I am convinced that the difference in the breadth of awareness and knowledge between the ant realm and the human realm is far exceeded by that between us and God.

However, there are major differences in the relationships. Ants all look alike to us; they have no apparent uniqueness, and we have no problem exterminating them just because they are a nuisance or have invaded our homes. They are of little importance to us and we consider them pests.

On the other hand, God knows each human being individually, the thoughts in our hearts, the number of hairs on our heads. We can also be pests. Many times in biblical history, God has wiped out people groups because of the evil in their thoughts and actions, but he is also infinitely patient and forgiving. He does not need any of us to accomplish his divine ends, yet he chooses to use us. Psalm 8:3–4 says it all: "When I consider your heavens, the work of your fingers, the moon and the stars, which you have set in place, what is mankind that you are mindful of them, human beings that you care for them?"

The fact that the Creator and Sustainer of the universe cares about me as an individual and loves me with an infinite love prompted the writing of this song.

"Still He Cares"

He formed the universe from nothing
He holds the earth and stars in place
Still he cares for me, yes he cares for me
His Word commands the powers of nature
From far beyond our time and space
Still he cares for me, yes he cares for me
Wonder of wonders the Maker of all
Would ever consider one so fragile and small

Chorus
Our God is so big
Our God is so great
There's nothing in heaven and earth he can't do
Still his passion burns bright
For his people it's true
He still cares for me, he still cares for you

His kingdom will endure forever
The angels bow before his throne
Still he cares for me, yes he cares for me
He charts the course of history
His truth and wisdom stand alone
Still he cares for me, yes he cares for me
How can it be that the King of all kings
Could carry a burden for such an unworthy thing

Bridge
He lives beyond the limits
Of the universe we see
Yet he promises to also live
In the hearts of you and me

How Do We Respond?

For what God has done for us, we should glorify
him in all that we do and live lives of *selflessness*, *humility*,
and *obedience*. I have aspired to this, although there will
always be much room for improvement.

- *Selflessness,* or dying to self, is a process that
  begins the moment we are born again and
  continues throughout a lifetime of sanctification. "Therefore, if anyone is in Christ, the
  new creation has come. The old has gone, the
  new is here!" (2 Cor. 5:17). Some elements of
  becoming a new creation are conveyed by the
  following lyrics:

"A New Creation in You"

When I look back on the one that I was
Before I walked into your light
There was no purpose, there was no cause
I was lost like a child in the night
But you took ahold of my body and soul
And offered a new kind of sight

Chorus
So thank you for taking
The old self and making it new
A new creation in you

No longer under the burden of sin
But under the freedom of grace
All the uncertainties living within
Gone without even a trace
Doubt and fear still try to enter this heart
But find that there's no longer space

Bridge
The old me is gone now
The past long forgotten
I hardly remember a time
When I wasn't yours
And you weren't mine

All the old passions, the needs, and desires
Now seem to be so far away
Trusting your promises, strong in your word
Nothing will lead me astray
Finding my purpose in living for you
And dying to me every day

- *Humility* is one of the greatest attributes of Jesus that we can emulate. On earth, he did not seek the privileges of his deity. He went from reigning in heaven to being lowly and unknown on earth. The Creator became the created and divested himself of deity to become one of us. He undertook our limitations, and at the end of his time on the earth, his humility turned to humiliation, as he was crucified as a criminal so that we could live.

C.S. Lewis said, "True humility is not thinking less of yourself; it is thinking of yourself less." And Jonathan Edwards said, "Nothing sets a person so much out of the devil's reach as humility." For an example of humility in the real world, consider the following story from over two hundred years ago about a corporal and a general.

> As he rode along, the general saw a group of men endeavoring to lift some timber. They were shorthanded, and the work was not going well. Their corporal stood by and repeatedly yelled orders at them. The general passed and said, "Why don't you lend them help and put your shoulder into it?"

> "Why sir," said the lofty corporal, "I'm a corporal, I don't do that sort of thing." The general got off his horse, pulled off his coat, and helped move

the timber; and by his efforts, the soldiers achieved their task. Then, he turned to the high and mighty corporal and said, "Mr. Corporal, next time you want a man to do such work as this, you can send for me. My name is George Washington."[6]

There are many Bible verses that deal with humility, but I believe that Philippians 2:3–4 sums it up: "Do nothing out of selfish ambition or vain conceit. Rather, in humility value others above yourselves, not looking to your own interests but each of you to the interests of others."

- *Obedience* may sound demanding, but it isn't meant to be difficult or burdensome. Two of my favorite verses, one from the Old Testament and one from the New Testament, are the following:

> "He has shown you, O mortal, what is good. And what does the Lord require of you? To act justly and to love mercy and to walk humbly with your God" (Mic. 6:8).

> "Love the Lord your God with all your heart and with all your soul and with all your mind. This is the first and greatest commandment. And the second is like it: Love your neighbor as yourself" (Matt. 22:37–39).

Interestingly, in God's economy, we're most fulfilled and happiest when we are looking out for others and not ourselves. Our supreme life objective and act of obedience, as the following song lyrics suggest, is to love.

"Heartbeat of Love"

Everybody has a power
That's in the choices we make
We can fill each waking hour
With either give or take
Whichever captures the heart and mind
Will set the course that we're on
And if we never make room for love
Pretty soon it'll all be gone, but if…

Chorus
We live love and we breathe love
Then our hearts will beat love every day
And soon the heartbeat of love will make
This world a better place

Selfish living is a downward spiral
It only makes the heart ache
Let's choose love now, take it viral
And watch the difference it makes
There'll be changes in everyone
We encounter each day
But more than that it will change the heart
Into a godlier place, 'cause when…

Bridge
Feel the heartbeat of love
Live the heartbeat of love

***

To conclude this lesson, God has every right and the wherewithal to do to us what we do to ants. But he chooses otherwise. We have no personal knowledge of or relationship with the ants, but the God of the universe knows more about us than we know of ourselves.

He has known you not only since you were born, but since eternity past. Imagine knowing the course of history from beyond time and space as we know it. Yes, God knows right now and has always known whether you would become a believer. He chose me, and if you have believed or will believe, he chose you. We don't deserve this special consideration, and we can't even begin to understand it. Just like the choice of Israel, choosing us was certainly not because we merit his choosing.

One of the great spiritual mysteries is predestination, along with God's divine option to choose. Many cannot accept that a hardened criminal, after a lifetime of wrongdoing, could have been chosen for glory in advance of time and attained it by accepting Christ on his deathbed. In our corrupted view of right and wrong, just and unjust, this doesn't seem to fit. But God is God. Ultimately, his will is what really matters. It is not about you and me; it's all about God!

LESSON 10

The Word of God Is Accurate from Start to Finish

I have quoted the Bible throughout the previous nine lessons learned as my ultimate source of truth and guidance. I'm sure skeptics who have not yet closed, given away, or thrown away this book (or deleted the digital version from their Nook or Kindle) must now be saying to themselves that this guy's entire argument relies on the accuracy of a book that doesn't align with historical and scientific facts and that contradicts itself again and again.

Let me address the latter first because I'm going to spend zero time on the subject. If you want a reference that exhaustively explores thousands of supposed inconsistencies within the Bible, I recommend John Haley's *Alleged Discrepancies of the Bible*. The open-minded reader will come away realizing that there are actually no inconsistencies at all. I do recommend this as a morning read because it will probably cure any insomnia you have if taken in at bedtime.

The Bible Is Accurate, Except for...

As mentioned before, I became a Christian in the biblical sense in my late teens, and for the next forty years, I believed the Bible—well, most of it. I would say I trusted the historical account of the Old Testament (from Genesis chapter 12 on) to be reliable and the books of the prophets to be truly prophetic. Of course, I believed the Gospels, the historical book of Acts, and the letters of the New Testament; my faith relied on their correctness. The book of Revelation was a bit confusing early on, but I had no doubt that the current dispensation would come to an end and that this book dealt with that time frame, the ensuing period, and the hereafter.

The trouble I had with acceptance of the historical and scientific accuracy of the Bible as a whole dealt with the first eleven chapters of Genesis, which did not seem to align in any way with the secular view of earth history that I had been exposed to since I was a very young child when, for the first time, I was introduced to dinosaurs.

Why This Is Important

If you are a believer, you might want to ask, "What's the big deal and why have you devoted so much space and energy in your book to this topic? The essential thing is that people come to Christ for salvation, correct?"

Yes, salvation is what ultimately is important. The big deal is that this is not what's happening. Generations of young people, many of whom are brought up in Christian homes, are encountering books and instructors in school and college asserting an ancient earth and evolution as fact. Many are rejecting Christianity, abandoning it if they believed early in life, or, in the best case, questioning their convictions and becoming jaded or lukewarm in their beliefs.

Many are rejecting the Gospel because the early chapters of Genesis lay the foundation for the Gospel, and if these chapters are a myth, maybe the Gospel is as well. Here is the very simple message of the Gospel from Genesis to Revelation:

- In Genesis chapter 1, on days one through six, God performed his work of creation; and in verse 31, he pronounced it all good.
- In Genesis chapter 3, sin and death entered the world through the disobedience of Adam and Eve, and what God pronounced good in chapter 1 was cursed.
- Also in Genesis 3 (verse 15) comes the first mention of sin's remedy—the Gospel of the coming Redeemer—where God says, "And I will put enmity between you [the serpent or Satan] and the woman, and between your offspring and hers [Jesus Christ]; he will crush your head, and you will strike his heel."
- In the New Testament Gospels, this promise is fulfilled through the crucifixion and resur-

rection of Jesus Christ as an atonement for sin
and to conquer death.

- In Revelation, Jesus returns, the curse of
  Genesis 3 is lifted, and all things are made
  new.

The problem with a multibillion-year-old earth, whether part of an atheistic viewpoint or a compromise position such as theistic evolution or progressive creation, is that bloodshed and death would have preceded sin, and God's pronouncement that his creation was *good* would have been erroneous. Death before sin negates the need for Christ's sacrifice or, at the very least, waters down the Gospel message.

The Age of the Earth and Evolution Lies

First, let me acknowledge once again the pioneers of thought and action in dispelling the myth of an ancient earth and evolution. I have mentioned some of them in my acknowledgments, but there are many. And more scientists and engineers are joining the ranks of young earth creationists every day.

For the last century, we have been bombarded by the idea of a multibillion-year-old earth from the moment we could grasp knowledge. There are hundreds of picture books for preschoolers about dinosaurs, and almost all of them, within a page or two, talk about these ancient animals that lived millions of years ago. How can any fertile mind not accept what is in published writing? As I grew older, the published writing documenting an ancient earth with ancient creatures became science textbooks, magazine articles, and journals—this viewpoint being corroborated by the media, museums, and the national park system. Science must have irrefutably proven that the earth was billions of years old if such a historical account was so widely accepted, correct?

Yet the first eleven chapters of Genesis state that the heavens and the earth—the sun, stars, and planets; the plants and animals; and human beings—were created by God in six twenty-four-hour days and that if you trust the genealogies in the subsequent chapters to be accurate, this six-day period was only about six thousand years ago. A couple thousand years later, God caused a global flood to cover the world and destroy everyone save a few, requiring the procreation of mankind to start all over again. Apparently, the human race didn't learn its lesson because several generations later, people decided to make a name for themselves by building a tower to the heavens. Again, God intervened by scattering the people and confusing their language, which is why I still can't understand Russian, Japanese, or Swahili. At long last in chapter 12, along comes Abram, and the Bible's historical account starts to fit the timeline most people believe.

Six thousand years versus 4.5 billion years—this is an irreconcilable dichotomy. Didn't the dinosaurs die out sixty-five million years ago? Didn't it take millions of years for the Colorado River to carve out the Grand Canyon? Doesn't it take millions of years for the light from distant stars to travel to the earth? How could man evolve from apes in just a few thousand years?

If the first eleven chapters of Genesis are allegorical and not historically and scientifically accurate, might there be other historical or doctrinal inaccuracies in the Bible? Are the moral absolutes of the Bible perhaps not so rigid? Might even my belief that Christ is the only way to God be based on a misunderstood teaching in the scriptures?

Before this lesson learned, I was having a bit of a faith crisis. I struggled trying to reconcile what the Bible said about the origins of the earth and life with the history I had been led to believe was confirmed by science.

Then, while walking to lunch one day several years ago, a friend and coworker suggested a few books and websites that might help lessen my confusion. This began a journey of ongoing study and investigation that has convinced me, without a shadow of a doubt, that God's Word is 100 percent scientifically and historically accurate and trustworthy, including Genesis 1 through 11. I cannot express how much my faith has been strengthened by this incredible epiphany. The short discourse that follows will not attempt an exhaustive exploration of the subject, but I hope that a few highlights of my discoveries will encourage those still influenced by a Satan-prompted lie of a multibillion-year-old earth and molecules-to-human evolution to reconsider their loyalties.

What Is the Definition of Science?

The answer to this question is foundational to reconciling the age-of-the-earth and creation-versus-evolution debates. The *Merriam-Webster Dictionary* says that science is the "knowledge about or study of the natural world based on facts learned through experiments and observation," the key words being *experiments* and *observation*. My degree is in science and engineering, and I am the first to admit that conclusions derived through observational science are irrefutable. If you can touch it, feel it, and experiment on it with reputable methods, it is probable that results are scientifically accurate.

Many people mistakenly believe that science has proven the earth to be billions of years old and that life evolved from a single cell, which in turn came from an accidental mixing of chemicals. This conclusion is based on observations about an unobservable past. Some call this historical science, which isn't science at all.

It's Not About the Evidence; It's About the Worldview

No human living on the earth today was around six thousand years ago, let alone billions of years ago, to observe the origin of the universe. So by definition, theories about what happened way back when are derived from analysis of the evidence that remains today: things such as fossils, the geology of the earth, astronomical features, and the genetic composition of life. I submit that analysis of this evidence shouldn't be classified as a faith-based approach versus a scientific approach, but by two opposing approaches to examining the evidence—one influenced by a biblical worldview and one influenced by a naturalistic or humanistic worldview.

I will say that when I run into a so-called old earth phenomenon that stumps me, my ultimate source of truth is the Word of God. After all, he was there at the beginning and has documented the way it happened. But as time goes on, there are fewer and fewer of these phenomena that I cannot refute with a logical explanation based on my biblical worldview.

Ten Evidences of My Choosing

After years of examining this subject, it has become apparent to me that 1) there is no factual evidence supporting an ancient earth and evolution and 2) the evidence that exists today is better explained by a model based on creation and a global flood.

Since this is a book grouped by tens, this section has ten examples of evidence that I consider compelling in support of number 2 above. I trust that interested readers will do some research on their own, and I guarantee you will find equally fervent interpretations of evidence on both sides of the debate, supporting each of the incompatible perspectives—old earth and evolution versus young earth and creation.

However, one thing is clear. The competing philosophies are not a subjective religious belief in creation versus an objective scientific believe in evolution. Rather, the competing philosophies are the biases of Christianity and humanism interpreting the same evidence in vastly different ways.

For infinitely more detail on this subject, I again refer you to the book *In Six Days*, in which fifty PhD scientists—geologists, biochemists, geneticists, etc.—give their reasons why they believe in a literal six-day creation roughly six thousand years ago. These individuals are not pastors, evangelists, or seminary professors; they are experts in their unique scientific fields, and they are all passionate in their convictions.

Again, it's all about one's worldview, and I leave it up to the reader to make his or her own judgment. But here are a few of the reasons I believe that in the debate about origins and history, the evidence is on the side of creation:

1. *When Dinosaurs Roamed the Earth*—This is a great topic to start with because I will have many people laughing out loud when I assert that dinosaurs and humans lived together only thousands of years ago. After your laughter subsides, please note that soft tissue—blood vessels and hemoglobin—were recently discovered in a T-Rex bone. Likewise, soft tissue was found in a Triceratops horn. Scientific evaluation of this evidence based on a biblical worldview suggests that these animals did not live millions of years ago since it is impossible for soft tissue to be preserved in fossils for anywhere near that long. Those with a naturalistic worldview have proposed a theory based on iron molecules in blood extending the preservation of soft tissue for millions of years, which does not seem plausible and has been empirically disproven.

    A much more controversial finding is the alleged discovery of human and dinosaur foot-

prints together in the limestone beds of the
Paluxy River in Texas, thought to be 120 million years old. Even evolutionists admit that
such an occurrence, if verified, would support
the doctrine of creationism. Therefore, anti-
creationists have devoted significant attention
and resources to ridiculing and distorting this
evidence.

By the way, the word *dinosaur* wasn't even
invented until 1841, yet depictions of these
animals can be found in all sorts of pictures
and drawings, including cave drawings, all over
the earth. What were they called before 1841?
Some called them dragons. But aren't dragons
mythical? If they are, why would eleven symbols of the Chinese calendar be based on real
animals and the twelfth (the dragon) be mythical? The book of Job refers to a similar creature as behemoth, an herbivore with a tail the
size of a large tree. Sounds like a Brachiosaurus
or Apatosaurus (formerly Brontosaurus) to
me. You might wonder: if Noah took two of
every animal on the ark, including dinosaurs,
wouldn't they be much too big? Well, even the
dinosaur population had infants, which started
out sufficiently small to fit in the ark.

2. *The Remnants of Catastrophe*—As an Arizona
    resident, I love visiting the majestic and awe-in-
    spiring Grand Canyon. However, everywhere
    you go in the Grand Canyon National Park,

the visitor center displays, placards, docents, and rangers make the commonly accepted claim that the canyon was cut by the Colorado River over millions of years. Yet if this was the case, certain phenomena are inconsistent. How is it that the headwaters of the Colorado River are lower in elevation than the plateau through which it seemingly cut? How was the breadth of the canyon and its side canyons carved by such a narrow meandering river? Where was the one thousand cubic miles of erosion debris deposited and where is it now located? There are no good answers to any of these questions.

As you might have already guessed, I believe that the Colorado River is the result of (not the cause of) the Grand Canyon's formation, which I believe resulted from various manifestations of the receding waters of the Genesis flood. There are certainly unanswered questions about formation specifics, but the evidence indicates it was formed rapidly by a lot of water rather than over eons of time by gradual river erosion.

We can see the potential for rapid and catastrophic erosion in recent geological formations, such as the fifteen-thousand-square-mile Channeled Scablands in eastern Washington, initially thought to be formed by a gradual process but recently proven to be caused by a glacial flood.

No one, however, appreciated the rapidity of catastrophic earth feature formation until the aftermath of the Mount St. Helens volcanic eruption of 1980, when mudflows carved their way through unhardened sediment layers resulting from the eruption. The result was what some call the Little Grand Canyon, a one-fortieth version of the Grand Canyon, with a remarkably similar appearance.

3.   *The Geologic Column or Time Scale: Nowhere in the Real World*—Further on the subject of geology, there are a few things to note about the standard geologic column (or time scale), which is the theoretical classification system for the cross section of rocks and fossils through the earth's crust.

First, it doesn't exist anywhere in the world the way it appears in textbooks and on websites. No matter where on the earth you look, layers that are pictured in the below diagram are nonexistent or out of sequence.

Second, believe it or not, the classification of strata in the geologic column was first devised by creationists to affirm the catastrophic process that created the geologic features we observe today. It was only after evolution became popular that the geologic column took on all of this theory's baggage.

Third, a number of evolutionists openly admit that the fossil record is damaging to their cause. Those who remain committed want you to believe that the column is somehow a picture of 4.5 million years of earth history. They support this contention with circular reasoning, determining the age of the rock layers by the fossils they contain, then turning right around and assigning the fossils ages based on the rock layers in which they are found. The evolutionist looks at the geologic column and sees more primitive ancient animals in the lower layers and evolutionary progress being exhibited the higher and higher one goes in the column.

GEOLOGIC TIME SCALE

ERA	PERIOD	EPOCH	SUCCESSION OF LIFE
CENOZOIC recent life	QUATERNARY 0 - 1 Million Years Rise of Man	Recent Pleisto- cene	
	TERTIARY 62 Million Years Rise of Mammals	Pliocene Miocene Oligocene Eocene	
MESOZOIC middle life	CRETACEOUS 72 Million Years Modern seed bearing plants. Dinosaurs		
	JURASSIC 46 Million Years First birds		
	TRIASSIC 49 Million Years Cycads, first dinosaurs		
PALEOZOIC ancient life	PERMIAN 50 Million Years First reptiles		
	PENNSYLVANIAN 30 Million Years First insects	Carboniferous	
	MISSISSIPPIAN 35 Million Years Many crinoids		
	DEVONIAN 60 Million Years First seed plants, cartilage fish		
	SILURIAN 20 Million Years Earliest land animals		
	ORDOVICIAN 75 Million Years Early bony fish		
	CAMBRIAN 100 Million Years Invertebrate animals, Brachiopods, Trilobites		
	PRECAMBRIAN Very few fossils present (bacteria-algae-pollen?)		

I and other creation advocates see the column hierarchy as a matter of sorting during the Genesis flood, with simpler and less mobile species at the bottom of the column and more advanced and mobile animals higher in the vertical column. Because the floodwaters didn't reach their maximum for one hundred fifty days after the start, you would expect organisms to die at different times based on the elevation of their habitats, migration during the early days, and even their intelligence.

There is one other frequently observed phenomenon that evolutionists have a hard time explaining: when an artifact of life such as a fossilized tree or a dinosaur neck is discovered vertically penetrating many layers of strata supposedly deposited over millions of years. In the context of evolution, there is something very wrong with that picture!

4. *Radiometric Dating*—There is an excellent book on this subject by Dr. Don DeYoung called `Thousands...Not Billions*, which challenges the results of radioisotope dating that shows the age of the earth to be billions of years. This book is almost textbook-like in its detail and depth of subject matter, but it provides compelling evidence that bad assumptions in radioisotope dating (for example, initial sample conditions and constant nuclear decay rates) have resulted in gross errors in sample dating.

    Here is just one finding to consider. Carbon-14 has a half-life of 5,730 years, which implies that any material over one hundred thousand years old should contain no Carbon-14 whatsoever. Yet in recent years, appreciable amounts of Carbon-14 have been found in fossils, coal, and diamonds. This is true for samples from the geologic record that contain fossils with presumed ages of hundreds of millions of years. Carbon-14 presence in these materials is clearly on the side of a young-earth view of history.

5. *Astronomical and Earth Phenomena*—Here are a few concepts within this topic I strongly believe are inconsistent with an ancient universe:

- Earth-Moon Separation: The moon is currently getting farther away from the earth at a rate of about 1.5 inches per year. Physics equations on the moon's recession over time that consider the earth's rotation rate, tidal forces, and gravity would put the moon touching the earth about 1.2 billion years ago, several billion years too recent for the believer in a 4.5-billion-year-old earth. A six-thousand-year-old universe would put the moon about seven hundred fifty feet closer to earth, which is not a problem.

- Existence of Comets: In the context of a multibillion-year-old universe, comets are relatively short-lived artifacts. Based on their matter loss rates and the fact that no new ones are being formed today, no comet should last more than a few million years. Yet they still abound in our solar system.

- Low Number and Small Size of Observable Supernova Remnants (SNRs): A galaxy like the Milky Way produces roughly one supernova (exploding star) every twenty-five years. The rate of expansion of the debris cloud can be predicted by physics models. If the universe were ancient, we should be observing thousands more supernovas and the cloud debris from those we see should be much bigger, but observations are much more in line with a younger universe.

- Earth's Magnetic Field: The magnetic field of the earth is caused by electric currents within its core. Measurements of this field since the early 1800s have indicated a decay rate of approximately 5 percent per century, and archaeological measurements show that the field was 40 percent stronger in AD 1,000. Accounting for magnetic field reversals and extrapolating this rate backward in time, the field could not have been decaying for more than about twenty thousand years, or else the original strength of the electric current would have been large enough to melt the earth.

- Salt and Sediment: The rates of salt deposition into/removal from the ocean and the rate of sediment accumulation on the ocean floor are well understood. If the earth were ancient, the ocean should be much saltier and the sediment should be miles deep. Neither is the case.

- Spiral Galaxies: The inner and outer regions of spiral galaxies rotate at different speeds, the inner faster than the outer. After a half billion years or so of this rotation differential, they would be too tightly wound for the spiral features to be recognizable. Yet we still see many examples of spiral galaxies in our universe.

- Distant Starlight: One of the common objections to a relatively young universe is the "distant starlight" problem—light from distant stars takes millions or billions of years to arrive at earth at the speed of light, proving that the universe is at least that old. Discounting a supernatural explanation, which I do not*, there are scientific explanations, one of which is a principle from Einstein's theory of general relativity called gravitational time dilation, which proposes that time goes faster in the presence of lower gravity. If, in terms of starlight travel,

Distance (d) = Speed of Light (c) x time (t),

and distance and the speed of light are invariable quantities, time (t) is the variable that can explain distant starlight reaching the earth much faster.

*If God created the earth on day one and the stars on day four, he certainly could have created the stars' light to be present on the earth at the time of their creation. Also, seventeen Bible verses state that God has stretched or expanded the universe from its original size, which could also be part of a supernatural explanation.

6. *Population Growth*—If humans first appeared on the scene a million or so years ago, where are the trillions of people living or in graves? Looking at the math another way, if the population started with four people a million years ago, in order to reach our current population, it would take 33,000 years for every doubling of the population. Kind of slow growth, don't you think? The world population growth is much more in line with the Bible's historical account.

7. *Nonexistent Plant Fossils*—In many geologic formations, including those in the Gobi Desert and the western U.S., there is ample evidence for animals but little evidence for the plants to support animal feeding. How did the

animals survive over the eons of time without food? The lack of plant evidence suggests that the layers were not deposited over millions of years, but rather laid down rapidly during the biblical flood.

8. *We Still Have Continents*—Rain flows into rivers, and rivers flow into larger rivers, which ultimately flow into the oceans and seas. Based on current rates of erosion, the continents would be expected to erode down to sea level in about ten million years. Even if the continents could be restored by means of uplift or volcanic activity, there would still be time for one hundred or more cycles of erosion and renewal if the continents were 2.5 billion years old, as some say.

9. *The Uniqueness of Human Beings*—I love animals. I've had many pets over the years, and I am fascinated by their antics, their instincts, their rational faculties, their devotion, and their relational tendencies. However, I totally disagree with *Time* magazine's March 14, 1994 article *How Man Began*, which starts with the statement: "No single, essential difference separates human beings from other animals." Contrary to this statement, there are huge differences.

    We humans are totally unique in our ability to use language and logic, to show amazing creativity in positive and negative ways: contributing through art, music, business, science, and literature while, at the same time, engaging in horrendous pursuits of crime, war, murder, theft, and self-destruction. What other species suffers from addiction, mental illness, and substance abuse? What other species has a sense of morality and ethics, even though we often choose to ignore what we know is right? What other species engages in Bible-instituted practices of wearing clothing and getting married? Most importantly, what other species fellowships with its Creator through worship, prayer, and relationship? The answer to all of these questions is this: no other species.

We were uniquely created in God's image—with a spirit and conscience that transcend instinct, with an inherent sense of our Creator's existence and a desire to seek him, with a knowledge of right and wrong based on moral absolutes instituted by God and written in his Word.

Evolution is a flawed theory that would have you believe that we share so much common DNA with the apes that we have to be related when, in truth, what we share with the apes is a common Creator. In this context, mutual DNA makes perfect sense. Critics and supporters alike call evolution a theory because it has never been and never will be proven. Sir Arthur Keith, who wrote the forward to *The*

Origin of Species (100th Edition) admitted, "Evolution is unproved and unprovable. We believe it because the only alternative is special creation, and that is unthinkable." That doesn't sound like a very good reason to me.

By the way, the term evolution in this section refers to macroevolution, the transition from one species to a more advanced species or, across the scope of history, from molecules to human beings. I have no problem with the concept of microevolution or adaptations and improvements within a species.

Even Darwin saw the flaws in his theory. He hoped that in time, there could be found evidence of intermediate species because he knew life couldn't hop, skip, or jump from one species to another, but his hope was in vain. There is one absolute certainty about these so-called evolutionary missing links: they are still missing.

Scientifically, the theory just doesn't add up because it relies on key mutations (or copy errors) that are favorable and add information, thus improving and advancing the biology. However, no mutation has ever been shown to add information, just subtract information.

What this theory did to a world that was looking for an excuse to deny God was provide that plausible deniability. For those adamantly opposed to creation, which by the way was generally accepted as truth until this theory came along, or for those walking the fence, evolution became the justification for removing God from the picture of history and from their lives. Likewise, it became justification for self-authority. After all, if we are nothing more than evolved pond scum, who other than ourselves is to say what's right and what's wrong?

When people are so convinced that they are correct, they will do anything to rationalize their position, including contriving false evidence to defend their case or dismissing outright good evidence that disproves their case. Purported human ancestral remains (Piltdown Man, Java Man, Nebraska Man, Lucy, Orce Man, and Neanderthal) have been proven to be frauds, true apes, or true humans.

In his obsession with convincing people that evolution was true, German embryologist Ernst Haeckel concluded that the evolutionary process from single cells to human beings was mimicked by embryological development within each species. He intentionally developed misleading drawings as evidence of his belief in common ancestry—drawings which, in time, were proven fraudulent. Sadly, they still appear in some biology textbooks.

This trend of misleading fertile minds, either through honest naivety or intentional deception, has continued throughout the past seventy-five years or more as schools, museums, literature, public television, national parks, and governments have become standard bearers for the theory of evolution.

10. *God Says So*—I hope that the information provided in one through nine above might sway skeptics to the creation side of this contentious and emotional debate. However, no matter how compelling or uncompelling the evidence interpretation is, I will never leave the firm foundation of God's Word in terms of my convictions on the matter. Even if one or more of the evidences above were invalidated, I would still believe in the creation account of Genesis, simply because God says that's the way it happened.

As you have probably guessed by now, I have a song about almost everything, including creation. For the following song, there is an accompanying YouTube video, to which I have provided a link, should you be interested. You may find some light-heartedness and even humor in some of the lyrics and visuals in the video. But let there be no doubt, I am dead serious about the subject matter.

https://www.youtube.com/watch?v=eGumGoRETV4

"We Are Created"

Open up your science book, what do you read?
Five hundred million years ago
We crawled from the sea
Breathed the air, grew some legs, learned how to stand
A few more hundred million
To become modern man
Well if this story's true
Our lives don't make any sense
And I have yet to see a shred of real evidence
So I won't be misguided, I won't be deceived
It's how the Bible tells it that I choose to believe

Chorus
We are created in the image of God
Made with eternity set in our hearts
Don't be persuaded by the enemy's lies
Every life has purpose in the Father's eyes
We all are special in the Father's eyes

The devil's always on the prowl for minds to dupe
Into thinking life emerged from chemical soup
That we're just one step further
Than our mammal friends
And just like them we live our lives
And die in the end
But God said on the sixth day
He breathed life into man

A part of him in every human soul who has been
So don't tell me my predecessors swung in the trees
I don't buy it, never will, 'cause I am unique

Bridge
I believe that life on earth was heaven sent
And not the product of some cosmic accident
We all play a part in God's perfect plan
A reason to be for every woman and man

Bible Accuracy Beyond Creation

I have certainly hit the creation discussion very hard, but there are other areas where the Bible reveals many scientific truths long before they were discovered by humans and forecasts many events long before they happened. This should confirm the Bible's supernatural origin in any objective mind.

- The Earth Is Round and Floats in Space— Isaiah 40:22 says, "He sits enthroned above the circle of the earth." The Hebrew word for circle implies a spherical or rounded object. This text is dated several hundred years before Aristotle suggested that the earth might be a sphere. In the time of Columbus two thousand years later, some still believed the earth was flat. Job 26:7 says, "…he suspends the earth over nothing," a discovery not made by science until 1650.

- Blood Is Life—Leviticus 17:11 says, "For the life of a creature is in the blood." It wasn't until three thousand years later in 1616 that William Harvey ascertained that blood circulation is critical to life. Bloodletting was a common "healing" method until the late nineteenth century, a practice that led to many deaths by those who obviously did not believe that blood was life.

- Hygiene and Microscopic Diseases—Cleansing processes prescribed in the book of Leviticus, such as washing using running water to avoid the spread of contamination, did not receive scientific confirmation until the mid-1800s, when Hungarian Dr. Ignaz Semmelweis directed doctors to wash their hands between examinations in running water, not in stagnant bowls, resulting in a dramatic drop in the sickness and death rate.

- Meteorological and Hydrological Cycles—"The wind blows to the south and turns to the north; round and round it goes, ever returning on its course. All streams flow into the sea, yet the sea is never full. To the place the streams come from, there they return again" (Ecc. 1:6–7). "He calls for the waters of the sea and pours them out over the face of the land" (Amos 9:6). The concepts of hemispheric wind patterns and a water cycle of precipitation and evaporation back to the atmosphere are clearly implied by these verses, yet these processes were not understood by science until two thousand years later.

- Grass-Fed Animal Food Products—Modern agriculture methods have increased production by emphasizing grain feeds for domestic livestock. However, recent studies have shown that grass feeding results in food products that are rich in the fats proven to be health enhancing and low in the fats that have been linked with disease. When we switch from grain-fed to grass-fed meat, we are simply returning to the diet that is most in harmony with our physiology and that which the Bible suggested thousands of years ago: "He makes grass grow for the cattle, and plants for people to cultivate, bringing forth food from the earth" (Ps. 104:14). Beyond meat products, the Bible has much to say about diet and its impact on human longevity. Needless to say, we have gotten far away from the scriptures' guidance on healthy eating. For more, I recommend the book *The Bible Prescription for Health and Longevity*, by Bill Sardi.

- Messianic Prophesies—Jesus fulfilled over 350 Old Testament prophesies written many centuries before he was born. Just a few are the following: the Messiah would be born of a woman (Gen. 3:15), he would be born in Bethlehem (Mic. 5:2), a messenger (John the Baptist) would prepare his way (Isa. 40:3–5), he would come from the tribe of Judah (Gen.

49:10), he would be declared the Son of God (Ps. 2:7), he would be crucified with criminals (Isa. 53:12), and he would be resurrected from the dead (Ps. 16:10). The list goes on and on, with the probability of this many predictions coming true by chance being infinitesimal. And for those who may think that scripture editors who came after Jesus made it "look like" Jesus fulfilled prophesy, a complete book of Isaiah (with its twenty Messianic prophesies) was found as part of the Dead Sea Scrolls, and this scroll has been accurately carbon dated at between 335 and 122 BC.

• The Week as a Time Metric—We measure the passage of our lives by a calendar based mostly on astronomical events. The day is the period of the earth's rotation. The month is the period roughly defined by the moon passing through all of its phases. The year is the time it takes for the earth to travel around the sun. The week also plays an important role in our lives. It establishes our work schedule and, for some, our pay schedule. The week is the basic cycle for vacations, event planning, television programming, and so many other aspects of our lives. The week was established by God based on his creation blueprint: six work days followed by a day of rest, typically our Sunday. The existence of the week points to a believable and trustworthy Bible.

The Bible was written over a period of 1,600 years in different languages by over forty authors living in different lands, with different backgrounds and occupations. Yet it tells one harmonious and consistent story from beginning to end, much of it foretelling a future that had not or has not yet happened. This could only be possible if the entire book was the inspired Word of God, which I firmly believe it is.

★★★

To conclude this final lesson learned, I spent nearly forty years of my Christian life in a walk that was impacted by doubts about the total reliability of God's Word, specifically Genesis 1–11. It was easy to dismiss this distrust as something that was not critical to my faith and service and something I hoped I might understand better in the clarity of eternity. But in fact, it held me back from being *all in* for the Lord.

Since I have learned, through an open mind and committed study, that the early chapters of Genesis are scientifically and historically accurate, my faith has become more solid and steadfast in every way. And remember where faith comes from. This is God's work in me. This is why I have devoted so much attention to the subject in this book.

I admit that I am very opinionated on this topic. But with my deepest conviction, I feel I am right and that my opinions are backed by evidence and of course by God's Word. I am convinced that the secular beliefs of a multibillion-year-old earth and evolution of life (and ultimately human beings) from an ancient primordial soup are part of the biggest myth that has ever been foisted on the minds of humankind.

Countless souls will stand before the Lord one day blaming blind belief in this myth for their doubt about the truth in the rest of the Bible, including the most important part: the fact that Jesus Christ died and rose again so that their sins could be forgiven and they could enjoy eternity in his presence. Unfortunately, at that point, it will be too late.

With that said, if you don't believe a single word of my tenth lesson learned, you won't be excluded from heaven. One's eternal destination is solely based on his or her response to God's gift of salvation through his Son. However, it is a fact that the Church is losing more people from each generation because they just don't trust the accuracy and believability of God's Word. And can you blame them? Secular society has convinced them that Genesis 1–11 is fiction, and by extension, the rest of the Bible could be irrelevant as well.

I love the Bible. I've read it cover to cover many times in multiple translations, and I read part of it every day. Don't get me wrong, every word in every book is important, but with my newfound confidence in the Bible's total accuracy, I read two books with renewed passion—Genesis and Revelation—because they are the only two where for part of the books, creation is perfect. The curse of Genesis 3, which destroyed the perfect relationship between the first two human beings and God, is reversed in Revelation 21; and all its painful ramifications—suffering, struggle, and death—disappear forever.

EPILOGUE

What's the Point?

The epilogue comes at the end of a book, but I wrote this section early on because I wanted to make sure there was a purpose in these pages of writing. Some write books to articulate a scientific concept or discovery, some to tell the story of an influential life, some to document a monumental historical event, some to spin a good yarn, some to make money.

I wrote this book for a broad audience of believers and nonbelievers because I want to see everyone learn the important lessons of living a fulfilling Christian life. It took me most of my years to learn these lessons, and I wish I had learned them at an earlier age.

The first and most important take-away is for the nonbeliever. I would like to see you in heaven some day, and if it's not obvious by now, I take what the Bible says about how to get there literally and seriously. Accepting the completed work of Jesus on the cross as full and final payment for your sin is all it takes. It doesn't matter if your parents are Christians or you were raised in a Christian home or you were sprinkled as part of the infant baptism rite. It's up to every individual to make this all-important decision of acceptance.

I hope if you make it there, we will all celebrate our various promised rewards for lives of service. But first and foremost, you need to get there. And all it takes is a simple prayer to ask Jesus to forgive you and come into your heart. You don't even need to buy my take on the universe's historical timeline presented in lesson 10, although I believe it will strengthen your conviction.

The more I see what's happening in the world today, the more I am convinced that my plea carries some urgency. First, no one is promised tomorrow. How sad it would be to recognize the truth but wait one day too long to ponder its significance and take action.

Second, there are very few, if any, Bible prophesies left to fulfill before Christ's promised second coming. Interestingly, even the secular community recognizes this anticipated event. In the newspaper world, typeface so large that it screams the headlines is called "second coming" typeface and is reserved for events such as the end of World War II, the assassination of JFK, or the World Trade Center attack.

Now I'm not going to be a fool like some end-time forecasters and try to predict when this is going to happen. The Bible says, "But about that day or hour no one knows, not even the angels in heaven, nor the Son, but only the Father" (Mark 13:32). But the very next verse says, "Be on guard! Be alert! You do not know when that time will come" (Mark 13:33). Note the exclamation points. I didn't add them for emphasis; they are in the Bible.

Part of being on guard and alert is being certain of your ultimate destination. Life on the earth is a brief blip compared to eternity, and everyone should aspire to be with God, not separated from him forever. As some say, we're all going to be dead a lot longer than we're alive, at least in terms of these earthly shells.

During the trial of Jesus two thousand years ago, Pontius Pilate asked the question, "What shall I do, then, with Jesus who is called the Messiah?" (Matt. 27:22). Little did he know he was asking the question of the ages—the question everyone who encounters Jesus must ultimately answer. Two verses later, Pilate made his decision. "…He took water and washed his hands in front of the crowd. 'I am innocent of this man's blood,' he said. 'It is your responsibility!' " (Matt. 27:24). Sorry, Pontius, it was your responsibility, just like it's each of ours.

Not one of us is innocent. We're all guilty, but the shed blood of Jesus has the power to cleanse us from our guilt and save us for eternity, as well as giving us power to overcome the world and live for God and others in the here and now. Are you walking the fence as you read these concluding words of the book? If so, I leave you with lyrics from one final "Come to Jesus" song and pray that this is your moment.

"This May Be the Moment"

Try looking beyond your fear
Know that there's someone near
To take all the weight away
Why carry the load alone
Making it all your own
Step out in faith today
Walk the path of trust only the heart can see
Be the one that God intended you to be

Chorus
This may be the moment
You've been waiting for so long
This may be the time to rise
And sing your victory song
Praising God for saving you
From emptiness and strife
This may be the moment
The greatest moment of your life

Time to lose all the guilt and shame
Jesus took all the blame
For all that you've ever done
Fly, spread out your wings and soar
Like you never have before
Into the arms of the Son
Say the words of faith you thought you'd never say
Realizing freedom's just a prayer away

Amen to those who have taken the first steps of acceptance and belief. Perhaps you are already laying it all on the line for the Lord. But if you're like me in my earlier years, you may *be* a Christian, but you're not *being* a Christian. You may know you're saved, but you're having a hard time putting the unsaved life behind. You may still be giving into temptation, focused on self, making earthly goals and possessions a priority, and saying *no* or *maybe later* to God's leading in your life. If this is you—and believe me, to an extent, it's still me—I pray some of my experiences will encourage and strengthen your walk. I leave the struggling or vacillating believer with the final lyrics of this book, a song I wrote a few years ago about letting go and allowing God to take control of your life. If you do, you'll never be the same. And that's a promise!

"Control"

So many roads ahead
Which to choose, where to go
Options can overwhelm
Which to pick, how to know
What course to be on
Till we turn to you
Then comes the clarity
Where to be, how to live, what to do

Chorus
Life makes much more sense
When you're in control
Uncertainty yields to a peace in our souls

The way is clear, there's no fear
Our world is whole
When we let go and put you in control

It's in our DNA
Wanting to run the show
Living on our own terms
Free to come, free to go
Therein is the paradox
We're never free
Till we forsake self
To follow you, live for you faithfully

Bridge
The lesson's a hard one
We're all prone to fail
But along the way some of us learn
That burdens are lifted
And spirits will sail
If we choose to follow you
Live for you, don't look back
Never return

"To him who is able to keep you from stumbling and to present you before his glorious presence without fault and with great joy, to the only God our Savior be glory, majesty, power, and authority, through Jesus Christ our Lord, before all ages, now and forevermore! Amen" (Jude 24–25).

REFERENCES IN TEXT

[1] http://www.conservapedia.com/Lionel_Luckhoo

[2] http://www.communicatejesus.com/40-quotes-life-changing-power-resurrection/

[3] https://w2.vatican.va/content/dam/francesco/pdf/apost_exhortations/documents/papa-francesco_esortazione-ap_20160319_amoris-laetitia_en.pdf

[4] https://www.youtube.com/watch?v=2-d4otHE-YI

[5] https://www.goodreads.com/author/quotes/56782.Loren_Eiseley

[6] http://www.angelfire.com/in4/jebaikeeam/ddd.html

ABOUT THE AUTHOR

Robert (Bob) Smith is a more complex person than his name would indicate. Fortunately, his parents gave him the middle name Dorsey so that he might be distinguished from 44,779 of the other 44,780 Robert Smiths in the United States. There is one other Robert Dorsey Smith in the U.S., who allegedly has a criminal record. This Robert is definitely not that Robert.

For the past seventeen years, this Robert has made a career of retiring and threatening to retire, though he will probably never fully do so. He retired from the Navy in 2000 after a twenty-eight-year combined active duty and reserve career in submarines. He actually relishes being called a bubblehead. In the same year, he left a small defense business he had helped grow, beginning in 1978. He retired from a large defense firm in January of 2015 and continues to pursue defense-related consulting efforts. As long as God gives the strength, it is doubtful he will ever stop serving the country he loves and to which he has given so much over the course of his career.

In the midst of a successful career in defense, Bob has pursued many extracurricular activities with passion and dedication. He is an avid writer of contemporary

Christian songs, swims competitively in senior Olympic events, and is an active leader of or participant in at least one mission trip a year. Bob was on the Academy Award-winning sound effects team for *The Hunt for Red October*, and his *Out of My World* CD was considered for the Contemporary Christian Album of the Year Grammy in 2013.

Bob currently is living in Tucson, Arizona and is eagerly waiting for California to fall into the ocean so he can own beachfront property.